How to Build a Better Pie

Sweet and Savory Recipes for
Flaky Crusts, Toppers, and the Things
in Between

Millicent Souris

Quarry Books
100 Cummings Center, Suite 406L
Beverly, MA 01915

quarrybooks.com • craftside.typepad.com

First published in the United States of America in 2012 by
Quarry Books, a member of
Quayside Publishing Group
100 Cummings Center
Suite 406-L
Beverly, Massachusetts 01915-6101
Telephone: (978) 282-9590
Fax: (978) 283-2742
www.quarrybooks.com

10 9 8 7 6 5 4 3 2 1

ISBN: 978-1-59253-796-9

Digital edition published in 2012
eISBN: 978-1-61058-396-1

Library of Congress Cataloging-in-Publication Data
Souris, Millicent.
 How to build a better pie : sweet and savory recipes for flaky crusts, toppers, and everything in between / Millicent Souris.
    p. cm.
 Summary: "You want to make pie, but are petrified of the crust. How can I get it to roll out and stretch over mounds of fruit? Will it tear, flake, burn, break, and disintegrate beneath my fingers? What about the filling: how do I get my custards to set, my blueberries to jell, and my meringues lofty and perfectly browned? Consider your questions answered and your fears alleviated. Millicent Souris, pie mistress and kitchen muse, teaches you the skills and techniques you need to master the art of making pie - skillfully, flawlessly, and deliciously. How to Build a Better Pie includes detailed information on everything from kitchen know-how to using the best ingredients. You'll find illustrated preparation techniques for fruit fillings, custards, mousses, creams, meringues, and more, along with crust recipes and techniques including chilling, rolling, shaping"-- Provided by publisher.
   ISBN 978-1-59253-796-9 (pbk.)
   1. Pies. 2. Cookbooks. I. Title.
   TX773.S677 2011
   641.86'52--dc23
                                                                                           2011050145

Design: Laura McFadden Design
Page layout: Claire MacMaster, barefootart.com
Photography: Greg Vore/www.gregvore.com
Cover design: Rockport Publishers

Printed in China

A Pie is Just a Pie

A pie, more than anything else, is an idea, a concept, a vessel for the desires of its creator. Whether you're trying to conjure nostalgia and memory, or just trying to bang out a dessert for unexpected guests, pies are as much or as little as you want them to be.

I suppose you could make a similar argument about omelets or sandwiches or alcoholic beverages for that matter, except pies don't suffer from any class warfare issues or have any residual stink left on them from trying to be elevated.

In a food world that is more and more being set upon and consumed by manifold sources of complete and utter b.s., pie remains good, safe, and whole.

Inexplicably, pie has survived in a culture that can even turn something as simple as barbeque or an egg into an haute cuisine fetish item. Pie is unassumingly the Teflon Don of things you put in your mouth by being indivisible from its simple charms and remaining all it ever was: pie.

—Tom Mylan

Tom Mylan is experienced in butchering, specialty foods, cheese, and local and sustainable sourcing. He is Co-owner of The Meat Hook in Brooklyn, NY.

CONTENTS

Let Them Eat Pie

I started making pies in 2001 in Portland, Oregon. I had moved there the prior year from Chicago on a whim, in hopes of finding some sort of peace or calm that I thought the left coast held. If it did have such restorative qualities, they did not suit me.

A redneck inspired me to make pie. My friend Matt Stark, Oregon born and bred, covered in tattoos, had never been across state lines, told me about an apple pie he made at his grandma's house one weekend. This blew my mind. He was a big, rowdy, dreamy fella who checked IDs at the bar where I was cooking.

This man made a pie. So I made a pie. My first pie was banana cream. I found the recipe in a James Beard cookbook, the kind of book whose spine literally hangs by a thread and its golden years are spent in a plastic bag that keeps it together.

I was taken with pie. It didn't require a lot of ingredients and I could afford to make it. It was deceptively simple with a lot of variations. Matt made it approachable merely by making it. I had always cooked for a living. By "cooked," I mean frying chicken at the convenience store, making sandwiches at a lunch counter, flipping eggs in college—jobs in the food industry. They were the kind of jobs when you smell like grease and squid and sweat at the end of a shift. But I had never baked before. I held baking, as many do, in the pantheon of cherub-cheeked nanas and holier-than-thou housewives and hostesses, people whose halos glitter with a special pixie dust the rest of us are not privy to. There were no family standards to aspire to, no precious recipe or handed-down pie crust tips. More importantly, there was no nostalgia or sentiment hindering me from making pies. There's a freedom to do your best work when there is nothing to lose. So I made pies—lots of them—sometimes two a day. Why make one when you can just as easily make two or three? There is always a willing audience for pie.

Since then I have made thousands of pies and tried every method I have read about. I've set quite a few ovens on fire, smoked out many a kitchen and taken a broomstick to more smoke alarms than I can count. I like to think I've learned some things from my numerous failures.

Here's the thing: People love pie. Even if it is not as perfect as you want it to be, people will eat it. And, when it truly, truly sucks, you have created a lesson for yourself. Our failures are as important, if not more so, than our triumphs in learning, so pay attention. It's worthless, both to your time and money, to just shake your head and damn yourself if your end result doesn't live up to your expectations.

What Pie Is and What Pie Isn't

This is not a book in which you find yourself deep in the pastry section of a kitchen supply store looking for molds, tweezers, and gold beads. We will never purchase foil tin cups or a piping bag attachment in the course of this book. These are promises.

"If you can grow it, pick it, kill it, or skin it, you can put it in a crust and bake it."

Pie is not cute or darling or maternal. It's a flaky crust filled with something sweet or savory then baked. It's as old as the hills—simple and classic. Every culture has its own version of pie.

Let's get back to pie as a utilitarian food, rather than a precious baked good that strikes fear in people. Some people are talented cooks, but everyone can learn to cook. You learn to do something because you must.

Sometimes a Pie Is Just Pie

When I started making pie, it was still just pie. Food wasn't as glorified as it is now. There weren't websites with restaurant gossip or civilians' reviews. People weren't talking about farms or footprints, and cooks were generally still just cooks. The food or restaurant world had fewer fetishes.

I teach classes on making pies. When I started teaching, I had an idea of what to emphasize. After teaching dozens of classes and hundreds of students, those ideas have changed. People tend to psych themselves out of making crusts and rolling them out. Making crust is simple—almost too simple. People overthink it. I can spot an obsessive-compulsive person by how they break the fat down in the crust, and I can tell what kind of self-loathing a person has as they roll out a crust. Let the simple be the simple.

Classic Recipe, Modern Touch

Food brings people together, around a table, at the market, across cultures, through decades and centuries. Pies have been around for a long time. I feel a connection with the past and people, a connection that only food offers.

The history of food mirrors the history of people. Pies were there at the beginning because they marry form and function. The crust acted as the container for cooking and the container for storage. We've evolved beyond the sheer necessity of pie, but we've been left with something incredibly delicious and versatile.

People's resourcefulness and shrewdness over time has led to some of the best food. The obstacles of poverty and lack of refrigeration have given us barbecue, smoked and confit meats, pies, pickles, and canned foods. Old recipes are a dialogue with the past. I believe there are more cooking secrets buried in the cemeteries of this world than in the most acclaimed kitchens in the biggest cities.

It's comforting to know that as sure as we are all born to die, something as little as a slip of paper with some instructions on how to prepare food can be passed along through time. We don't have to have children or enough money to name a hospital after ourselves or find a cure for something. We can just make food, and pass it along. That might be enough.

—*Millicent Souris*

CHAPTER 1

Putting the Pie in Your Kitchen

It doesn't take much to equip your kitchen to bake pies. That's probably why I took to it so quickly—it's not necessary to invest in a lot of kitchen equipment. When engaging in a really old cooking method, you'll find that the things you need are welcome additions to your pantry: It evokes a real "tried-and-true" approach. You do not need to special order anything here or find it in some far-flung corner of the world.

We don't seem to start with the basics anymore. There are a million cookbooks out there, and so many television shows, restaurants, and ideas swimming in our heads that we don't just start at the beginning. These ideas add different flavors, techniques, and flashy utensils, strange graters, and specialized pans and so on. Nothing equates to having a kitchen we can actually cook in. The following list addresses what you need to make pies and what you need to function well in your kitchen. These tools truly earn their keep in your kitchen drawers; rather than become clutter, these items are transformative for ease in cooking. You will always need mixing bowls and baking sheets. In fact, you probably don't even understand yet *how much* you need them.

Allow me to introduce you to the beginning in hopes that it will cut down on scrambling in the middle and the end.

Putting the Pie in the Pantry

Pie plates. Glass pie plates are classic, and they conduct heat well and predictably. They enable you to spy on the bottom crust as the pie bakes to see when it's done. There are two different standards: one is 9 ½ inches (24 cm) in diameter, generally with two handles and a scalloped edge. The second is a 9-inch (23 cm) plate, slightly shallower, with a simple rim.

If you have metal pans, use them. You may have to shorten the overall baking time slightly, as metal is thinner and transfers heat faster than glass. Metal pie pans also tend to be a bit shallower, so you may use less of the filling called for in the recipe.

Wooden rolling pin. Wooden rolling pins are superior to all other options. Marble pins are too heavy for pie crust, and silicone rolling pins are messy: The crust sticks to the surface. Wooden rolling pins are well balanced, affordable, clean up

THESE LITTLE BIRDS HELP TO PIPE STEAM OUT OF YOUR PIE, PUTTING THE *FUN* IN FUNCTION.

and store easily, and allow you the control needed to roll out the crust. (Look for vintage wooden rolling pins at thrift stores, yard sales, or flea markets.) French rolling pins are also excellent; instead of handles, they just taper at the ends.

GLASS PIE PLATES

Aluminum foil. This kitchen staple does more in this world than wrap up your leftovers. Aluminum foil should have a musical written about it, I love it that much. Foil is a fantastic heat shield for a crust as it bakes. It also can be used to line the bottom of your oven, catching any drips of butter, fruit bubblings, or other detritus from baking. Foil heat shields are reusable. I marvel at how quickly it cools, too. You can handle it right out of the oven.

Baking sheet. Bake juicier numbers on it (as a tray for your pie plate) or place it on the rack below the pie to catch drips. Even if you forsake making pies forever, a good baking sheet will always have a use in your kitchen. I recommend aluminum sheet pans (called half sheets in restaurants); they are 18 x 13-inch (45.7 x 34 cm) and fit in most standard ovens. Please buy a rimmed one so all liquids remain safely contained on the tray and do not spill into your oven.

Microplane grater. One of my favorite tools in the kitchen is the Microplane grater. It is truly a transformative tool, as nothing zests citrus or grates nutmeg or ginger like it. It enables you to add delicate flavor to your food, where perhaps before your lemon zests were too large, pithy, and clunky.

Bench scraper. A tool that I have recently let into my life is a bench scraper. Metal ones are strong and stiff and clean a flat surface like nobody's business, but rubber ones conform to the inside of a bowl and can scrape clean your rolling pin too.

Bowls. Nothing does the job like the correctly sized bowl. Invest in at least two medium-size bowls. What is medium size? The diameter should be bigger than a classic LP—12 inches (30.5 cm). For a true test, see if you can put both your hands in the bowl with some wiggle room. With good bowls, your life in the kitchen will sort itself out easier than you can anticipate.

MICROPLANE GRATER

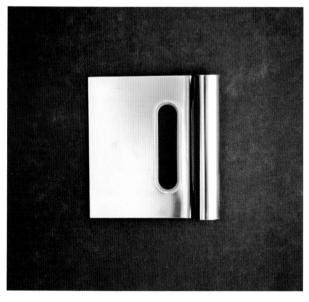

BENCH OR BOARD SCRAPER

GOOD-SIZED BOWL

DRY MEASURING CUPS AND SPOONS

LIQUID MEASURING CUP

Measuring cups and spoons. How else are you going to measure things? Solids and liquids require different measuring cups.

Kitchen shears. You never know how great kitchen shears are until you use them. Buy a pair. They give you the most control with trimming your pastry ends. Beyond that they can accomplish an astonishing number of tasks. You will wonder how you've gone without.

8- to 10-inch (20 to 25 cm) cast iron pan. You don't own a cast iron pan yet? It is the least expensive, most useful investment you will ever make...in and outside the kitchen. A cast iron pan will last many lifetimes. They can be purchased new or found used. They hold heat better and more evenly than any other vessel in your kitchen. Try making pot pies in them.

Baking beans. Take the name quite literally. Use a bag of dried beans (any style). These are used to weigh down your crust during blind baking so the crust holds it shape. They are very important. They can be reused until they turn rancid.

Here's a quick list of some odds and ends that will be helpful in your newly stocked kitchen:

Pastry brush for delicately washing the crust

Pasta cutter to make lattice strips

Pie bird to elicit steam from the inner depths of your pie

Parchment paper for a multitude of uses. Not aluminum foil or cling wrap, parchment is great to line your baking sheet for an easier cleanup.

While not essential for your journey into pies, they're good, uplifting, and functional.

Pie-Making Tips

Cooking scares people, and baking scares a lot of people. Pies are an intersection of the two. These tips come from a few things: answering questions during classes, having an obsessive mind, and running kitchens are the main three.

As we have moved further and further away from knowing how to cook we have lost our grip on common sense. Some people don't even enter the kitchen anymore, while others rely on faith, any kind of faith, rather than science. Cooking isn't a miracle, so you just need to arm yourself with the best weapon: information.

Reading Recipes

Always read an entire recipe before you begin. This cuts down on the number of surprises. Trust me, it helps.

Handling Heat

Using an oven thermometer is the only way to find at what temperature your oven actually runs. Ovens rarely are true to the temperatures they claim, so adjust your baking temperatures up or down accordingly.

Do not stick your finger in a hot pie out of the oven. Hot sugar can really burn you, and hot sugar mixed with the sticking properties and viscosity levels of hot fruit will bring you much pain. Your freshly baked pie needs to rest; it benefits from time for the juices to redistribute themselves and become reabsorbed. Let your pie cool for at least an hour after baking. Fruit pies need to sit longer. It's a hot mass. Let's not make it a hot mess.

Minimizing Mess

A good way to help form and maintain the shape of your pie once it has been sliced into is to take wax or parchment paper, fold it lengthwise to at least an inch (2.5 cm) thick, and place it in the pie pan, pressing it against the exposed edges of the pie. Use it to move some seeping filling back into the rest of the pie. It is astonishingly strong.

Keep a piece of aluminum foil on the bottom of your oven to catch any drippings (butter, fruit, syrup, etc.). This will still cause smoke to come out of your oven when you check your pie. Sadly, that is what cooking at high temperatures does. The payoff is worth it.

Place your pie on a rimmed baking sheet to catch any spills. Just put the sheet in the oven during prebaking so it heats up too. The baking sheet adds another layer of insulation against the heat for the bottom of your pie to bake. If you place the baking sheet on the rack right below the pie, it allows heat to have a more direct contact with the bottom rather than if it's sitting on the baking sheet.

Eggs

Eggs are almost the perfect food. You can spend a lifetime thinking about eggs, talking to different people about how they cook them, marveling at their ability to be all things to all people. Eggs can be breakfast, lunch, dinner, or dessert. They can even be a beverage. Eggs are brilliant.

The apparent quality of all food changes when you make a concerted effort to purchase food made and raised with an intention of responsibility and flavor. Eggs are easily the most affordable protein. Even if you buy a dozen farm-fresh eggs for three times the supermarket price, it is still the protein with the best value. Just crack open an organic or pasture-raised egg and look at the yolk to understand the difference.

If you shop in a big supermarket, it is generally best to buy organic eggs which are controlled under government regulations and must adhere to certain standards. If you have a local market or farm stand, ask how they keep their chickens. Some are certified organic, and some are pasture raised. Pasture-raised opens a can of worms of antiregulation, but when you find the people who are raising their animals to the spirit rather than the loose letter of the idea of pasture-raised, it is worth it.

The terms *cage-free* and *pasture-raised* aren't held to government regulations, so we must hearken back to the days of knowing where our food comes from. Beautifully pasture-raised eggs reflect the seasons as the chickens are pecking about on the land, so at the peak of growing season the yolks are the most decadent sunset orange and continue to be. Then they lessen a bit in the winter as the land and the meals change.

Pasture-raised eggs have more vitamins and less cholesterol and saturated fat than supermarket eggs. Unlike fruit, eggs do not get more flavor as they age. The fresher they are, the better they are.

Dairy

By-products of sad animals are things you do not want to ingest, and dairy is no different. There are reasons why food is expensive, and to bend it to fit our will, as we have done with factory farming, has not made the world a better place. And it has not actually helped people.

When you bake with eggs, milk, buttermilk, or heavy cream, they should be at room temperature. Just as it is important to preheat your oven, it is important to bring your food out of the cold. For liquids just measure them and leave them out; it shouldn't take more than an hour for a cup of dairy to warm up. With eggs you can leave them out in the shell or put the

raw eggs, in the shell, in a container of warm (not hot) water to take the chill off. Since the shell protects the egg, it will keep it cooler longer. Temperature is really important when baking. Prebaked crusts must cool down before they're brushed with egg white to fill any holes and give them a sheen. If the crust is too hot, the egg white becomes opaque. The same goes for any pie filling that has eggs in it. The crust should be room temperature and the filling should too.

Eggs and the lovely custards they create do not like to be baked at high temperature. I always partially bake any crust for an egg-based pie and allow the pie with the filling to bake at no higher than 375°F (190°C, gas mark 5). Using curdled eggs for pie filling is an unappetizing affair.

Sweeteners

You can always tell if you need more sugar in a pie before you bake it. The sweetness shapes the flavor, almost like salt, of what you're baking.

Think of sugars as colors. Basic granulated white sugar is just a sweetener. It has a very transparent, one-note flavor. It allows blueberries to be blueberries, just adding enough sweetness to boost their flavor. It is basic and affordable.

There is a point with white sugar where it starts to taste like processed food. I like to use brown sugars to balance tartness (such as apple, rhubarb, or tomatillo). It lends a depth to flavor. Light and brown sugar are really white sugar with added molasses, but what molasses adds is a world unto its own. The warmth of brown sugar rounds out the tartness of some fruit, such as rhubarb.

Sometimes a mixture of white and brown sugars is ideal, because while white sugar lends the basic sweet, something darker adds another layer of sweetness.

Molasses is a tricky beast to bake with. It's quite viscous, as is honey, and can affect the color of your pie. I have used molasses in pumpkin and sweet potato pie, but it creates a burned-looking top, so try to avoid it.

The dark horse of sweeteners, the one that is possibly sitting unbeknownst to you, is maple syrup. It lends a gorgeous, mysterious depth to a pie. It isn't too thick, and it has its own unique flavor. It's not necessary to use a lot of it either. Add just a shot to a cherry pie or apple pie. (Add it to a blueberry pie, if you dare add any more liquid to that juicy beast.)

Maple sugar is also a wonderful thing, albeit more expensive and harder to find. It is created from maple sap, boiled down to the sugar crystallization point; hence the price. It is sweeter than regular sugar.

The sugar I like most to sprinkle on sweet pies' top crusts is turbinado sugar. Less-processed, it has a larger grain than regular sugar. (If you don't have turbinado sugar, white sugar is fine, but don't use brown sugar; it's too influential on the color of the crust.)

Crust Wash

Good food works all of the senses. As much as the highs and lows of flavor affect food, so does texture and color.

Baked goods should not look the same coming out of the oven as they did going in. We eat with our eyes, and a rich brown, caramel-like color is inherently appetizing. It's akin to a sear on a steak or crispy roasted chicken. It's a sensory indication that the food will be nourishing and delicious.

A wash is something you put on a baked item, whether that is bread, a biscuit, or a pie crust. Adding a wash to your pie crust is a sure way to maximize the sensory reaction.

Your choice of wash is versatile; it can be a whole egg, an egg white, an egg yolk (diluted with water), milk, half and half, or heavy cream. The richer the wash, the richer the color. If you brush some skim milk on the top crust, it will be lighter than egg yolk.

If you find it wasteful to use a whole egg as a wash on a pie crust, then don't use it. You have options. If your filling, or some other part of your meal, uses egg yolks, then use the egg white, and vice versa. If you don't have any eggs around then just use some milk.

Thickeners

Fruit pies need thickeners. Cornstarch, the most common, is a bit oppressive as a thickener,. It clumps easily, and if you do mix it with water first, you're just creating a paste, which is a bit unseemly to put with your lovely fruit. Isn't it a pity to do all this work to make a pie, and then put in two tablespoons of cornstarch that may be intrusive to all your work? The world of thickeners is a vast one, so I suggest the following:

Flour—all-purpose, pastry, or cake—is a great go-to thickener. Tapioca and arrowroot are also reliable—just make sure they are ground.

Ground white rice is also an excellent thickener for pie filling. Whichever thickener you use, remember that it must be used in tandem with time. Fruit pies need to sit and rest; they retain heat far longer than you imagine. A pie out of the oven an hour later is still steaming in the center. When the filling is really hot, it cannot set; it stays hot and runny. The filling needs to cool for it to firm up. Thickeners can thicken juices, but only time can set a pie.

- -

Think of food as a balance, a song, where you need the high end but also the low end. Sugar is not just sweet but a slight depth of flavor that doesn't encumber the flavor of the fruit but adds a treble to it.

- -

CHAPTER 2

Crusts

Pie crusts are primitive beings: flour, salt, and sugar with chunks of fat barely held together by water. The faster you are able to mix all these ingredients and shape them into a crust, the better. With such simple recipes it is paramount to measure well, have the ingredients at the temperatures called for, and to work quickly.

But it can take a while to achieve a deft hand, so keep in mind that practice, practice, practice is the key to success. Get your brain out of the process, do not overthink it, and just allow it to be the simple act that it is.

Over time, many home cooks have gotten away from mastering the fundamentals of cooking to prepare specific recipes. Some recipes are ideas about flavor. Some are about skills. Making pie crust is a skill. You have way more command in the kitchen when you can execute something without a recipe. Once you master a kitchen skill, you can move on to the next skill, whether that's breaking down a chicken or making a roux. That's the best part of cooking; it's a lifetime of learning.

With all skills comes the awkward learning period where the moments of failure appear to outweigh the victories. Perseverance is important. Even if you feel like your pie crust is disastrous, if you keep on, you will most likely get a pie at the end of the day. Sure, you could go out and buy the rolled-out crust, but that's called cheating. And it's not good crust anyway.

Luckily the world is full of willing people to sample your journeyman pies. Everyone should add more of a restaurant-world attitude toward their cooking: Failure is not an option.

Old-School Recipes for Modern Times

The glory of old recipes is their versatility. Back in the day, true homesteaders certainly didn't have the patience for fussiness; their food was about practicality and adaptability. It is an amazing approach to food that erases sentimentality and certainty and focuses instead on solid foundations of cooking.

Ingenuity still rules. You don't need a pie pan or the necessary amount of filling to create something; you can always make turnovers.

This chapter's crust recipes are all made by hand. No pastry cutter, no bread knives, no blender, no food processor. Doing it by hand is the fastest, cleanest way to make crust that gives you the most control, and it's the easiest to clean up. There are many useful tools out there in the cooking world. Your hands are two of them.

Basic Pie Crust

2¼ cups (280 g) all-purpose flour

3 teaspoons (18 g) kosher salt

2 teaspoons (8 g) white sugar

2 sticks (224 g) cold unsalted butter

½ cup (120 ml) strained ice water,
plus 2 to 3 tablespoons (30 to 45 ml)

mixing bowl

fork

plastic wrap

This is an amazingly versatile recipe for a double-crust pie. It can be used for sweet or savory pies. It can be all butter, all leaf lard, all shortening, or any combination. For savory pies you can even use beef suet. Choose a good-size bowl, one where both of your hands can fit in and work. You will be mixing the crust with your hands. Pour all dry ingredients into the bowl and mix together in the bowl with your hands.

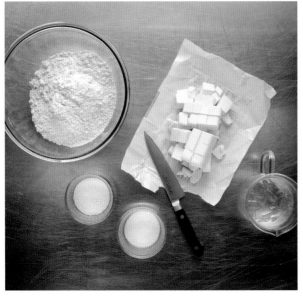

1 Choose a good-size bowl, one in which both of your hands can fit in and work. You will be mixing the crust with your hands.

2 Pour all dry ingredients into the bowl and mix together in the bowl with your hands.

3 Cut the cold butter into ¼-inch (6 mm) pieces. It is very important that your butter be cold; its ability to maintain its shape is what lends flakiness to the crust. You can freeze it, but I find refrigerated butter to be quite sufficient.

4 Scatter the butter over the dry ingredients. Incorporate the butter into the dry ingredients by pinching each piece. Do not break up the butter beyond this; it should keep its shape. You are really just introducing them to each other.

5 As you work, cup your hands and lift all the dry ingredients from the bottom of the bowl to the top. Do this a few times so you aren't stuck with dry ingredients at the bottom of the bowl. (The butter should not get warm or create tiny little butter pebbles. The goal is for the fat to have presence in the crust. It has a lot of work to do; leave it some backbone.)

For a Single Pie Crust, follow Basic Pie Crust recipe using these measurements.

- -

Single Pie Crust

  1 cup (125 g) and 3 tablespoons (24 g) all-purpose flour
1½ (6 g) teaspoons kosher salt
  1 teaspoon (4 g) granulated sugar
  1 stick (½ cup) (112 g) cold unsalted butter
 ¼ cup (60 ml) strained ice water, plus 2 tablespoons (28 ml)

- -

6 Strain the ice water so ice doesn't end up in the crust. (Ice water is used for the same reason cold butter is: to keep the fat separate through the process.) You can also pour the ice water through a slotted spoon held over the bowl.

7 Slowly pour the water into the bowl. Start with ¼ cup (60 ml) of water, and pour it around the outside of the bowl. Never sloppily dump wet ingredients into dry ingredients, especially for a crust. The water should be evenly distributed. Push the crust around with the fork, moving from the outside of the bowl. Add the second ¼ cup (60 ml) of water and repeat.

Why the fork? Why the pushing? Pie crust has the best texture when it is worked the least. When you push it around with the fork, you are not mixing it, stirring it, or kneading it. You are just pushing it. The more you work it, the tougher it becomes. Your pie crust should be tender, not tough.

8 When mixing the ingredients, make sure you are incorporating all ingredients on the bottom of the bowl. You've added ½ cup (120 ml) of water. It is almost there, but you probably need to add at least 2 tablespoons (30 ml) more water. After adding the extra water, push the crust more with your fork.

Note: In warmer months you may not need the last tablespoons (30 ml) of water because of the humid air. Always slowly add water to a crust before adding any more. Once you add it, there is no going back.

Now, a splash of water from your fingertips or a dusting of flour can tip the balance in the crust texture. Say your crust is almost together but just needs a little shove, or it's beginning to feel a bit tacky. Try just a touch of water or flour to adjust the texture.

Shaping the Crust

Your crust is ready to be shaped when a few things occur:

- You can squeeze it together and it won't fall apart, and the center is not just a crumbly, dusty mess. And, please, you are *squeezing* it, not kneading it. It's not bread or pasta dough, it's pie crust. Quit touching it!

- The crust becomes slightly golden and a little cooler to touch. This is the perfect moment when the mixture becomes *crust,* where the equilibrium between the dry ingredients and butter has been achieved.

Yield: 2 crusts (5-inch [12.7 cm] disks, before rolling)
Prep time: 5 minutes

9 Separate the dough into two equal-size balls and flatten them into disks. (For this recipe, the disks should be about 5 inches [12.7 cm] in diameter.) Wrap each one in plastic wrap and refrigerate them for at least 30 minutes before rolling them out.

And that is how you make crust.

How Goldilocks would have taught you to make pie crust

TOO DRY　　　　　　TOO WET　　　　　　JUST RIGHT

Fat: Variations on a Theme

Each pie crust uses ½ cup (112 g) of fat. The fat can be butter, but it can also be shortening or lard. Many recipes call for a mixture of shortening and butter, with the idea that shortening adds flakiness while butter adds flavor.

Pie-making mythology debunked: Butter can add flakiness, too. A certain percentage of butter is water, somewhere between 15 and 17 percent, and when it is baked at a high temperature for a short time, the water steams out of the crust, creating flakiness. Butter makes flaky biscuits, croissants, and puff pastry, so it will definitely do it for your pie crust.

Shortening adds a cleaner flavor to your pie. It's great with delicate fruit.

Leaf lard has a flavor similar to shortening. Leaf lard is a visceral fat deposit in the pig, located around the kidneys and by the loin. It may seem counterintuitive to use animal fat in sweet pies, but leaf lard creates an excellent, versatile crust.

The essential lesson: Fat is interchangeable. The Basic Pie Crust recipe can be altered by what you have on hand: shortening, butter, or leaf lard. You may use just one or a combination of the three. There are reasons for each of them, and sometimes that reason is necessity. Please, let's get back to a time when necessity counts as a reason, too.

My bottom line: The volume of fat in this recipe is a constant. You fill it with the flavor you wish.

How to Freeze Your Crust

Yes, you may! Wrap the flattened disks of dough well in plastic wrap and store them in your freezer. They will be usable for two weeks. (I encourage you to use common sense, however: If your frozen crust appears to be covered in freezer crystals, pitch it.)

Thawing your crust properly requires some advance planning. Ideally, pull it out of the freezer the night before you intend to make the pie, or at least 3 hours beforehand and put it in the refrigerator. Do not try to thaw it faster on the counter or by the stove. The dough will be too warm on the outside and still frozen on the inside, thus making it completely maddening to roll out.

Pie crust lasts in the refrigerator for an indefinite amount of time, but it begins to oxidize after a few days. Your best bet is to use pie crust no later than three days after making it. If that's not going to happen, freeze it.

If you make some, don't freeze it and forget about it and then find it, look at it closely. Do you want to eat it? In general food tells us if we want to eat it. A good rule of thumb is this: If you feel repelled by it, leave it alone.

Crust and Intuition

As with any new skill, you need to learn to balance achievement and perfection. When I started making pies, I found that a lot of recipes call for a minimal amount of water. If you don't truly understand how to put pie crust together, you won't see what is absolutely essential for its success.

At its simplest, all crusts must roll out. If you think the crust needs a little more water to hold together, you are probably right. If you squeeze your crust together but the center doesn't hold, you won't be able to roll it out.

Ingredients' temperature is very important when making pie crust; it affects how you make it and how it rolls out. You need to incorporate the cold fat into the dry ingredients quickly so the fat does not melt. If your kitchen is warm, put your dry ingredients in the freezer or refrigerator until you mix the fat. Add ice water (strained) to the mixture at a slow rate so you can monitor the level of moisture. This part always takes longer than you think it's going to.

- -

Kitchen Essentials: Unsalted Butter, Kosher Salt

Always use unsalted butter in cooking and baking. It gives you control for seasoning your final dish. Never buy salted butter, unless it's some insanely delicious salted European butter, but you should be eating that raw, not baking it into things. Please, just cut to the chase and purchase a box of kosher salt for your kitchen. Not the alleged sea salt towers from your local supermarket, not the drums of iodized salt. Kosher salt. Use it for baking, cooking, and even rubbing on meat.

The salt in the Basic Pie Crust has a definite flavor presence, not just texture. Salt does not make food salty; people make food salty. Salt enhances flavor. That's why wars were fought over it.

- -

Rendering Animal Fat

When you render animal fat, you are taking the skin, such as duck skin, a fat deposit, like the pig's leaf lard, and exposing it to heat. The lard melts out of the skin or deposit, leaving you with two things: the actual fat, which is liquid when it is hot, and crispy cracklings, which once housed the fat. The process is very similar to frying bacon. A cast iron skillet is best for rendering; it absorbs and distributes the heat of the burner the most consistently and reliably.

Preparation of the Fat

Cut the fat into smaller pieces so more surface area is exposed to the heat, thus rendering more quickly and with a larger yield. Add about a cup of water, just so it shallowly covers the bottom of the pan to help move this along. The fat pieces won't scorch before it starts giving way. Along the way the water evaporates out of the fat. Render fat over low heat—you do not want to burn it. When you cook fat too high, you burn it, and once you burn something, you cannot go back in time and unburn it.

The duck skin or leaf lard is rendered when the original chunks are crispy, golden, and hard. There is no more fat in them. Strain them out and store the liquid gold in the freezer so it solidifies.

After thirty minutes you have fat, cracklings, and no water. You just need a bit of water and a dependable pan to render fat.

Fat Crust

1 cup (240 ml) water

2 ¼ cups (280 g) all-purpose flour

3 teaspoons (18 g) salt

2 teaspoons (8 g) granulated sugar

1 cup (200 g) cold rendered duck fat
or 1 cup (200 g) cold bits of beef suet

½ cup (120 ml) strained ice water
plus 2 or 3 tablespoons (28 or 45 ml)

mixing bowl

fork

plastic wrap

Mix together your dry ingredients in a bowl that both of your hands fit in easily. Sprinkle bits of beef suet over the flour and toss throughout. If using duck fat, quickly use a spoon to make tiny, stone-size pieces to scatter over the flour. Rendered duck fat is very soft. Regardless of the fat, quickly incorporate it into the flour, making sure to lift up the dry ingredients on the bottom of the bowl. If it feels like the fat is getting too warm, put the bowl in the freezer for 5 minutes.

Add ¼ cup (60 ml) of the strained ice water and quickly mix with a fork. Add the remaining ¼ cup (60 ml) and mix again. If the crust is not coming together in the center when you press it together, add 1 tablespoon (15 ml) of water at a time. Stop when the crust can hold its shape as a disc. Make 2 flattened discs, wrap in plastic wrap, and refrigerate.

- -

Put an Egg In It

As they do with everything, an egg also enriches a pie crust. The color becomes more golden and the crust is more solid. Whip up one egg for a single crust and add some strained ice water to liquefy it a bit. Add it first before other liquids, so it is spread out in the crust instead of concentrated in one place. Add more water as needed.

- -

UNRENDERED LARD

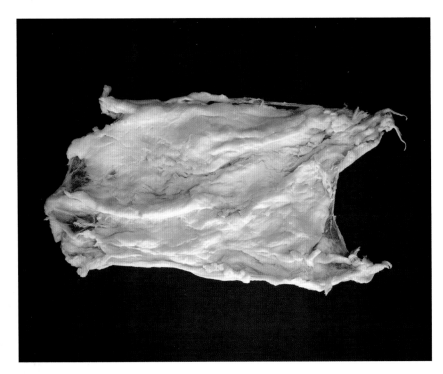

It's strange to think that a fat deposit from inside of a pig could be considered clean, but that's exactly what leaf lard offers: an almost transparent flavor that offers a flaky texture to crust. It counters well with the flavor of butter for any kind of pie and works well on its own.

WHOLE LEAF LARD

RENDERED LARD

Alternative Pie Crusts

There are more crusts options out there than you can shake a stick at. The basic pie crust can be transformed into a traditional pie, a turnover, the top to a pot pie, a pastie, or a hot pocket. This crust can also take almost any kind of fat, and while the ones covered in the previous chapter are versatile for sweet pies, this can handle a few other variations to go savory.

Baking with Animal Fats

Beef suet is the fat deposit found around the kidneys of a cow. It is classically used in British pastry. It's a very large structure of long pieces and crumbly fat pieces. There's no need to render the beef suet because it just crumbles into the pieces you need, albeit with a little help from a chef's knife. Clean it up by pulling it off the connective tissue (which acts and seems exactly as its same indicates) and cut out any red parts. Chop it up into small pieces and refrigerate them.

Cows are big. So is their fat.

Ducks have a lot of fat to give in their flesh; it's specific to their nature. Duck fat is actually more akin to olive oil than butter. It's also a readily available by-product from purchasing one duck. A duck is so fatty that you can butcher it down, cook the breasts and the leg, and break down all the fat from the carcass and render it. (Always check under the little duck armpits, there is a wealth of fat there.) Carve the fat off the backside of the carcass too, and the neck is the jackpot of fat.

BEEF SUET

Cheater Tops and Bottoms: Crumb Crusts and Crumbles

If you can make a crumb, you can make a crumb crust. The most classic crumb crust is the graham cracker crust. But there are so many other crumbs to be discovered in this world! The cracker section in the supermarket alone is a devastating example of selections created by capitalism, and any choice can become your next crust.

Once I was left with a cake fail, one that broke on its way out of the cake pan. It sat in the refrigerator getting stale, becoming less than delicious. I broke it up into crumbs and let it sit uncovered on the baking sheet until it became hard. The dried cake was perfect for a crumb crust.

I'm not suggesting you have to bake a cake if you want to make a chocolate crumb crust. I am saying that sometimes mistakes lead to something good, and this chocolate crumb crust was good.

A chocolate or vanilla wafer crumb crust can be achieved by just buying some snack bags of the vanilla wafers or cheap chocolate cake at the supermarket.

If the store-bought cakes are too moist, break them up into pieces with your hands and bake them at 375°F (190°C, gas mark 5) until they dry out, about ten or fifteen minutes. You can also just leave them out and let the air do the work, if time permits. You could also try chocolate crackers, if you can find them.

Savory Cracker Crusts

For savory pies you can make savory crusts. The one I stumbled upon and like is the saltine cracker crust. Saltine crackers perform well in the crust format because they are minimally processed. Other crackers are just too processed to perform the responsibilities of a crust.

When you experiment with cracker and crumb crusts, always keep in mind what the flavor of the original food is. Saltine crusts don't need added salt. Sometimes a chocolate crust does not need sugar. Taste the crust before you add sugar or salt to the mix. You didn't make the crackers yourself, so you don't know what they need until you taste them. Add an egg white as an additional binder.

Cracker Crumb Crusts for Sweet Pies

Using a food processor to make your crumbs will make a more even crumb than your hands. Break up the crackers and put in the food processor. Pulse the crackers until they break down. You don't want them to be dust, but you also don't want them to be chunky. You want crumbs. Keep the food processor running and add the melted butter, and then add the egg white.

1 ¾ cup (205 g) crumbs of your choice (graham crackers, vanilla wafers, chocolate cake, etc.)

1 stick (½ cup [112 g]) unsalted butter, melted and cooled a bit

1 egg white

¼ cup (50 g) granulated or packed brown sugar, or a mix

1 teaspoon kosher salt

9-inch (23 cm) glass pie plate

Preliminary Preparation

It's important that the butter is cooled so it does not inadvertently cook the egg white. Add the sugar and salt. If you feel like the crackers are sweet enough, add less sugar.

1 If you want to get really specific, and I do, I prefer the 9-inch (23 cm) glass pie plate to the 9 ½-inch (24 cm) pie plate with handles for crumb crusts. It's a bit more shallow for this smashed-together crust.

2 Empty your crumb crust into your pie plate. Tamp down with your open palm.

3 You want to press the crust down, but you don't want to make press it together so much that you create an impenetrable crust.

4 You also need to create the sides of the crust. I form them by using my thumb and index finger as a guide for the height of the edges.

5 The edges are no more than ½ inch (1 cm) up the sides of the pie plate; otherwise I find they don't keep their shape when you get the pie out of the plate. Put this crust in the refrigerator for at least 20 minutes. It needs some time to come into its own.

6 Preheat oven to 350°F (180°C, gas mark 4). Bake crust for 10–15 minutes.

Crumble Topping

I can call a crumble crust a cheater's crust, but the proof is in the pudding. This recipe comes from a woman with a real knack for crumbles: Kelly Geary (of Sweet Deliverance in Brooklyn, New York). Just because something is easier does not mean it is cheating.

In a medium-size bowl, mix together the granulated sugar, flour, salt, and oats. Toast your nuts and chop. Add your brown sugar and nuts to the bowl and mix everything together. Scatter the butter over the dry ingredients and incorporate it in like regular crust until it is crumbly. Hence the name.

I must say that a crumble is really quite delicious. Use it the same as a regular top crust. If during the cooking process it gets too dark, just put the aluminum foil shield on top to protect it. It's really chewy and mouthwatering. It makes a massive mound on the top of the pie and then cooks down.

You can also make batches of this and freeze it to use at a later date.

2 ½ cups (500 g) granulated sugar

2 cups (250 g) all-purpose or pastry flour

1 teaspoon kosher salt

1 cup (80 g) rolled oats

1 cup (120 g) finely chopped nuts: walnuts, almonds, or pecans

¼ cup (60 g) packed brown sugar

14 tablespoons (196 g) cold unsalted butter, cut into small pieces

Shortbread Crust

- 1 cup (125 g) all-purpose flour
- ¼ cup (50 g) granulated sugar
- ¾ teaspoon (4 g) kosher salt
- 1 stick (½ cup [112 g]) unsalted butter, softened
- 1 egg yolk

Eben Burr, longtime friend, turned me on to the joy and flexibility of the shortbread crust. It is more cohesive than the traditional pie crust and acts more like a cookie. Shortbread is a different beast, a fantastically delicious different beast that works a little easier than the classic crust.

Turn the oven to 400°F (200°C, gas mark 6) and place a baking sheet in it.

Whisk 1 cup (125 g) of flour, ¼ cup (50 g) of granulated sugar, and ¾ teaspoon kosher salt together. Add 1 stick (½ cup or 112 g) of room-temperature unsalted butter and an egg yolk. Mix with a wooden spoon or your hands.

Pat into a shallow 9-inch (23 cm) glass pie plate. Prick with a fork a few times and put in the refrigerator for 10 minutes. Line the inside snugly with aluminum foil and even out your baking beans on top. Place on the hot baking sheet in the oven.

Check after 10 minutes. Pull the foil up and see if the crust has set and become more cohesive. If not, leave the foil on for 5 more minutes. If it has, pull the foil and beans off and let the crust bake until golden. When it is out of the oven, immediately compress it with a wooden spoon. It helps to push back the sides anywhere it has sagged.

Cheddar Cheese Double Crust

This is an excellent crust for apple pie. Apple pie and Cheddar cheese may surprise some as an excellent pairing, but it is terrific and warms the depths. The hot cheese activates the salivary glands when the pie gets pulled from the oven, and its scent is beyond enticing. The sharper the Cheddar cheese, the more presence it will have in the crust.

2 ¼ cups (280 g) all-purpose flour

3 teaspoons (18 g) kosher salt

2 teaspoons (8 g) granulated sugar

1 ½ sticks (¾ cup) (168 g) cold unsalted butter (12 tablespoons fat)

½ cup (60 g) grated or thinly cut cold sharp Cheddar cheese

½ cup (120 ml) strained ice water plus 2 or 3 tablespoons (28 or 45 ml)

regular fork

plastic wrap

1 Choose a good-size bowl, one where both of your hands can fit in and work. Measure your dry ingredients and mix them together in the bowl. Cut your cold butter into ¼-inch (6 mm) pieces. It is very important that your butter is cold; its ability to maintain the integrity of its shape is what lends flakiness to the crust. You can freeze it, but I find refrigerated butter to be quite sufficient.

The cheese adds another element of fat to this crust, so you may not need as much water. Don't just pour the water in the same spot on the ingredients; you have to scatter it about. If the crust feels really wet just sprinkle a bit of flour.

2 Scatter the butter over the dry ingredients. Incorporate the butter into the dry ingredients by pinching each piece. When you incorporate the butter, it is meant to keep its shape—you're just introducing the two. You don't want your butter to get warm with the flour or create tiny little butter pebbles. The goal is for your fat to have presence in the crust.

3 Scatter the shredded cheese over the ingredients.

4 Quickly toss the cheese through the butter and flour. Make sure to get everything at the bottom of the bowl into the game.

5 Add the ¼ cup (60 ml) of the strained ice water along the outside of the crust. Mix quickly with a fork. Add the remaining ice water and mix with the fork or your hands.

CHEDDAR CHEESE PIE DOUGH

6 When mixing the ingredients, make sure all the little bits on the bottom of the bowl are incorporated. Separate the crust into two equal-size balls, and flatten them into disks. If they won't hold in the center, sprinkle a bit of water on the crust. If they feel a bit wet, sprinkle a bit of flour on the crust.

CHAPTER 3

Rolling Out

Rolling out pie crust is the real deal-breaker for people. It's what keeps the frozen crust people in business—the severed horse-head in the sheets, the last nail in the coffin. It makes people want to run away from pie making. Pie making is not hard. Making the crust and rolling it out are the hard parts. Rolling crust out is simple, and as with most simple things, the few things that are important are truly crucial.

For making pie crust there is plenty of white-noise advice out there on how to ease the situation. People without electricity or cars or college degrees have rolled out pie crust for centuries, possibly while perishing from consumption, and we think we need the latest tricks in a food magazine to accomplish it. Tricks are crutches; just eliminate them.

Learn to work quickly. Use chilled crust. Do not press down on the crust with your hands. After every roll turn the crust 90 degrees. If it sticks, scrape your surface and your rolling pin clean. Dust both with more flour. Do not bear down on your crust as you roll it out. It's simple. Just roll the crust out. Get your complicated brain out of it. This is a skill. Start learning it and you will get better each time.

Essentials for Rolling Out Crust

Chill: Chill your crust it for at least thirty minutes. You want a firm, solid crust. Sometimes I try to quicken the process and curse myself because the crust is difficult to roll out. By firm I mean when you take it out of the refrigerator, your thumb leaves a bit of a print when you press it and it is solid. Anything less gets difficult, especially in a warm kitchen. Do not compromise on this step.

Thaw: If your crust is frozen, it is important to thaw it properly, which means thawing evenly. Do not thaw it on the counter: The outside will be warm and the inside still frozen, making it impossible to roll out. If you pull the crust from the freezer and put it in the refrigerator the night before, the crust will thaw evenly.

Work surface: Choose the right surface in your kitchen to work. The best way to determine this is to put your rolling pin on the surface. Does it fit? Then use it. Have a small bowl of flour at the ready; it's your bench flour for sprinkling on the surface and rolling pin. If you have a bench scraper, by all means have it at your side. A kitchen towel is also handy.

Stay moving: Heat is the enemy of pie crust. It makes it difficult to work with—that is why you are always chilling it. Just as you want to cultivate a quick and deft hand at making the crust, you want to do the same with rolling it out. This is action, not thought. You should always be moving.

The Rolling Method

1 Sprinkle your board (where you are rolling out) with flour, just a small handful.

2 Pull your crust from the refrigerator and unwrap it.

3 Your crust should be in the shape of a flattened disk rather than a ball. It makes rolling it out easier.

4 I put my hand over the crust and give it a full turn in the flour. I'm not gripping it, I'm just barely holding. I want to get a feel for it. Has it chilled enough? Is it a bit dry or a bit wet?

5 Also when I do this the body heat from my fingertips are melding any cracks on the side. Remember, this is just barely held together.

6 I am also turning the crust a bit in the flour.

7 Now the fun begins. Give your crust a few good whacks with your rolling pin, but only if it's wooden. If the crust has chilled enough, it will respond well to the beating, flattening out at a quick rate.

8 I do this because it accomplishes a few things. If the crust has set enough and is cold enough, it won't stick to the pin. If it does, put it in the freezer for a few minutes. This beating also almost doubles the diameter of your crust with very little work.

(continued)

9 Begin rolling. Here is the pattern: Roll up and down—once. Rotate your crust a quarter turn. Roll up and down *once*. Don't bear down hard on the crust. You're just rolling it out, not pressing it out.

10 Rotate the crust a quarter turn after each roll. Then you know it's not stuck to the bench.

I first found the method of pounding the crust with a rolling pin while watching an old *Julia and Jacques* cooking show on public television. Jacques Pepin takes his rolling pin and lightly and politely taps his *pâte brisée* a bit. Julia Child picks up her rolling pin and just goes to town on the crust in the amazingly bravado manner that *was* Julia Child.

11 Roll up and down *once*.

12 Rotate your crust a quarter turn.

13 Roll up and down *once*.

14 A pie plate is circular. Machines make pie plates. Machines make circles. As humans we can only aspire to make circles. Try we must, though, and this is the technique where you try to do so. It gives you the most control to make sure you can get the shape you want from your crust.

Get the picture? This is how you roll crust out. This is the song in your head as you do it. Roll up and down—once. Move your crust a quarter turn. That's it.

And the following is what you are accomplishing as you do these very few, very basic things.

- When you roll up and down only once before you turn it, you are ensuring that you are not rolling the crust into the bench.

- When you turn it, you are checking that the crust is not sticking to the bench and you are creating the shape of the crust.

- The crust is being rolled out evenly, achieving the same thickness all around.

- To figure out if your crust will fit in the plate just place your plate on top of it and eyeball it.

WORK CLEAN

SEAL CRACKS

The Adjustments

Now that we've worked through the best method for rolling crust, there are some trouble-shooting examples that will help along the way. A few problems may occur as you roll your crust out, but hold fast and trust this information.

Work clean. If your crust sticks when you go to turn it, quickly move it to the side and use your bench scraper to clean the surface. This is very important. Fat sticks to fat, so any little smears of melted butter or lard or shortening on your board is going to stick to the bits in your crust. Make sure your rolling pin is clean too. If you have a malleable rubber scraper it can clean your pin, or use a clean kitchen towel.

In an ideal world you are motoring along and your crust is rolling out, you are moving it, and it is as humanly close to a circle as possible. Your crust may stick a bit, but you're cleaning the bench and your rolling pin and tossing some more flour on the surface.

Seal cracks. Try to pinch together any cracks as they come. In the beginning it is usually just around the outer edges of the crust, but sometimes you get a little crack inside. Pinch it together and roll over it. The crust will seam itself together. Remember: Fat sticks to fat. It works both for you and against you.

- -

Bench (or board) scrapers are fantastic tools. Not only do they clean up your board, they can separate any part of your crust that sticks. Slide the scraper under the crust where it is sticking to dislodge it. Scrape the board clean and dust with flour. Disaster averted.

- -

RESHAPE

If your crust shape is becoming something more akin to the shape of the continent of Africa rather than a circle, do not fret. It does not take much to guide the shape back into a circle. A few focused and concerted efforts to even out your crust with a roll here and there will pay off. Do not despair. You can fix it.

And here is the magic part of the recipe: the part that makes the recipe the recipe. This disk of pie crust you have made, once you have it rolled out to fit in your 9- or 9 ½-inch (23 or 24 cm) pie plate, about 15 inches (38 cm) in diameter, will be the thickness you need to bake it in the time given in the recipe.

RESHAPE

You want your crust to be evenly rolled out (another factor of the quarter turn), no less than ⅛ inch (3 mm) in thickness around. If you get it too thin, it's too much like a cracker in the pie plate, and your bottom crust has some work to do. If it's too thick, well, it won't fit in the plate.

The beauty of this method is that because you've just quickly rolled it out once and turned it each time, you have control over the crust. It is not stuck to your board. It is pleasantly dusted with flour, and you can flip half of it over the other half, pick it up at either end, and place it in the center of your pie plate, and unfold it.

When you do this once, you will understand the joy of this control. It's in the same vein of making the crust, quickly, with your hands, knowing what is happening to it every step of the way.

Centering the Crust in the Plate

When you put the crust in the plate you want to center it when you place it in, and then unfold it (a, b, c). Be very gentle with your crust; it is a delicate being. Lift the edges of the crust and let it set naturally in the plate. It should be flush with the plate, not stretched across from the bottom to the edges. Turn the plate and keep lifting all the edges, tucking it along the rim (d, e, f).

- -

If you don't have a rolling pin any good-size bottle will do. I can't remember my first rolling pin, but I know I used empty wine bottles quite some time ago. They're great because they're empty, and you can freeze them before use so they keep your fat cold.

- -

Trimming the Crust

Have a pair of kitchen shears ready or your sharpest, shortest knife (a). Trim the excess crust, leaving a ¼ inch (6 mm) of overhang from the edge of the plate (b). Now, with your thumb and index fingers (they are the real workhorses of pie making), lift and tuck the crust, gently pinching it to set along the rim of the outer edge of the plate. Turn the plate as you go (c, d, e, f).

If at any point you feel your crust becoming sticky, place it in the refrigerator to firm up for a few minutes. Once you have the crust trimmed and pinched, place your crust in the freezer or refrigerator. If you need to prebake the crust, ideally place it in the freezer before baking. It's really important for it to be level so the crust doesn't fall.

Patching Your Crust

Pie crust can be forgiving. If you have a tear in your crust when you put it in the plate, do not fret. You can easily patch it with the bits you have left over when you trim the edges. Going along with the fat-sticks-to-fat ethos that can mess up your life as you roll it out, the scraps happily stick to the crust to even it out, whether it's on the bottom or along the edges.

Keep your scraps, unless they are a big melted mess. You can use them for galettes or turnovers. (See page 58 for more on these techniques.)

THE FINISHED CRUST

Top Crusts and Fruit Pies

There are two kinds of fruit pies with crusts, ones with full top crusts and ones with lattice crusts. It's not just a matter of aesthetics—the two function differently. A lattice-top crust reveals more surface area of the filling, so it allows more liquid to evaporate from the pie. Lattice crusts are imperative to use for really juicy pies.

TOP CRUST
(OPPOSITE) LATTICE CRUST

I use lattice tops throughout the spring and summer when fresh, juicy fruit is in season. For me, the flavor of the pie is more important than having a solid center filling, where the fruit is almost more like jam. Using fresh fruit and less thickener are important to maximize the flavor, and I use the lattice top so the liquid filling can reduce more.

A full top crust is classic for apple pie. Apples have a lot of naturally acting pectin, so the pie filling doesn't suffer for the lack of reduction of the juices. I take any chance I can get to use a full top crust. It has a wonderful medieval nature.

Making a Lattice Crust

Simply, a lattice is a pattern. It is a pattern created by several strips of crust. It is no more complex than that. And here's how you make it.

Roll out your top crust like your bottom crust. About halfway through, roll your crust a little more into a rectangle shape. You don't need a perfect circle for the lattice. Take a knife or your pasta cutter and cut strips lengthwise. You may use a ruler to measure the width of the strips, or you may eyeball it. All your strips should be about the same width. The numbers of strips you have, and their width, determine your lattice. If you cut really thin strips and end up with fourteen in total, you are making a lattice that is seven strips horizontally and seven strips vertically, 7 x 7. If you cut really thick strips and end up with six in total, you are making a lattice that is three strips horizontally and three strips vertically, 3 x 3. If you end up with eleven strips your lattice will be five strips vertically and six strips horizontally, 5 x 6.

Each type of lattice is beautiful. The really thin strips are iconic, but if you are working in a very hot kitchen it is best to do thicker, and fewer, strips. They are also beautiful in a solid, less delicate way. The more elaborate lattice tops are just sadistic to execute sometimes.

You are doing this right before you plan on baking the pie. Remember, for raw crust heat is the enemy. This is the last part of your pie's assembly. Your filling and bottom crust should be ready, so have them ready. Your oven is preheated, and everything is a go.

- -

I started to do 3 x 3 pies in the July and August during one the hottest summers on record in an unairconditioned kitchen. The pastry handled better, it was less delicate, and the lattice was faster to make. The thicker strips also keep a better shape after cutting into the pie.

- -

1 Fill the pie and place it right above or below your top crust.

2 Pick up your lattice strips on both ends and start placing them vertically across your pie.

3 Let them sit on the fruit; do not stretch them across the top. Place them as equidistantly as possible.

4 Do not pinch the ends of the strips on the rim of the bottom crust.

5 Arrange the strips across.

6 Gently lift all the odd-numbered strips halfway up the crust. Place your longest lattice strip horizontally across the pie. Gently pull down the odd-numbered strips over this first strip.

7 Now, either below or above the next horizontal strip (I like to think of it as the anchor), pull up the even-numbered strips. Place your next lattice strip horizontally across the pie.

8 Gently pull down the even-numbered strips over the second strip. Pull up the odd-numbered strips.

9 Trim the top edge to meet the bottom edge.

10 Pinch the edges together to seam.

11 Lightly wash the lattice with egg or cream and dust with sugar.

1 Have your filling ready. Place your pie bird in the middle of a chilled, empty crust.

Making a Full Top Crust

A full top crust is a dream: easy to create, classic, and wonderful to look at. It also offers you the opportunity to use a pie bird. Pie birds are ceramic birds you put in the middle of your pie to conduct steam through the pie. A pie bird is a perfectly archaic, decorative, and functional object.

2 Place the apples around the bird.

3 It's good to spiral the apples so they all lie flat.

4 Your filling should not eclipse your pie bird. Make sure you get the other ingredients out of the bowl into the pie also.

5 Roll out your top crust exactly as you did your bottom crust. Fold it in half and place centered on top of the pie. Press over the bird's beak so it can break through the crust.

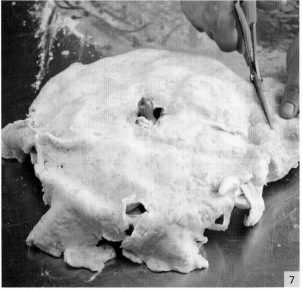

6 Lift the edges of the crust so it rests on top of the filling, rather than stretching over it. This texture is really lovely on the finished pie.

7 Trim the crust so it is flush with the edge of the bottom.

8 Pinch the crusts together. Use your thumbs and index fingers to scallop the edge, or just let your freak flag fly and leave it rough.

9 A full top crust must have slits in it to release steam as the pie bakes. Take your sharpest knife and cut through the crust in whichever manner you desire.

You do not need a pie bird to use a full top crust. Plenty of pies have gone on to lead happy lives without them. Treat your crust the same way. You cut slits in it either way.

Washing the Crust

Both lattice and full top crusts benefit from a wash of some sort, whether it is a whole egg, egg white, milk, or heavy cream. The wash provides an excellent texture to the baked crust and enriches the color of the crust too. I like to also sprinkle the top with raw sugar. The sugar also lends a lovely crunch to the top of the crust, and a delicious sweet aspect to it.

Hand Pies and Turnovers

The original intention for pies was a self-contained unit of food.
Nothing exemplifies this more than a turnover or a hand pie.
The crust is the edible container and the food is mobile and tidy.

There are two ways to make these pies: You may use one piece of crust and fold it over or you can use two separate crusts, where one is the bottom and the other the top.

To make turnovers: The single crust recipe makes three turnovers. Separate the crusts into equal-size balls to roll out. If you are making turnovers, you just need one crust for each pie. Roll the crust out to no thinner than ⅛ inch (3 mm) in a circle. Put your chilled filling in the top third of the crust and pull the bottom part of the crust over it.

To make hand pies: If you are making hand pies with a separate bottom and top, it is good to use a punch, something that will create same-size pieces so you waste less crust. This can be a biscuit cutter or the lip of a mason jar or a bowl. Roll your crust out like a regular pie crust, no need to divide anything into separate crust disks. Punch the crust out. Your filling will go in the center of one crust and then be topped with the other one.

The important thing to consider when you construct hand pies and turnovers is that the crust is the vehicle. You must leave an inch (2.5 cm) of untouched crust around the perimeter so the crust can be sealed. This seal is everything; it is what contains the unit. To seal the crust, use brush water or beaten egg on the bottom. Then press the top down over the filling, pressing the air out as you seal the edges. Just that bit of moisture, whether it is water or egg, and the firmness of your fingertips seal the deal.

Using Pie Scraps to Make Galettes

Inevitably there are bits of your pie crusts left over. It's just the nature of the beast, and while a more mathematical person may really calibrate the recipes so there is no excess, some days we just need the excess to fill the pie plate. The leftovers from rolled-out pie crusts can really haunt a person. The accumulation of leftovers over the years becomes especially haunting.

Here's the rub: You could save the leftovers from many pies and make one whole single crust, but that crust will be tough, and strange. And how long will it take you to save these leftovers? Unless you are making several pies every day, it will take a while.

A better use for these scraps is to turn them into galettes, which are freeform fruit tarts. Galettes are incredibly easy to make and serve as great desserts when you don't have a lot of time, or fruit, or people.

To Make Galettes

Press all your crust scraps together in a ball, cover with plastic wrap, and refrigerate. Don't knead them together or try to make them cohesive; just smash them together. Allow them to chill for at least 30 minutes.

The filling is dependent upon how many galettes you are making. Each galette requires about ½ cup (60 g) of filling, and they should not be overfilled.

1 Take your crust out of the refrigerator and pinch off a bit about the size of a golf ball. Lightly dust the surface with flour.

2 Roll the crust as you would any other crust.

3 You don't want the crust to be thinner than ⅛".

4 Make a stable bottom of fruit, especially if it is sliced.

5 Build up with your ½ cup (60 g) of seasoned fruit, leaving about an inch (2.5 cm) of crust around it free.

6 Lift up one of the crust edges over the fruit with your thumb and index finger.

7 The crust will rest on top of the fruit, then move your fingers down about an inch and pull that bit of crust on top of the fruit.

8 As you continue to do this, press together the crust as it intersects with itself atop the filling.

9 Keep doing this with all the crust edges. Then brush the crust with a wash, and sprinkle liberally with sugar. Bake at 425° (220°C, gas mark 7) until the crust is golden, about 25 minutes. Let cool for 20 minutes.

CHAPTER 4

Fruit Pies

I never knew how much people are seriously in love with pie until I ventured into fruit pies. Something about fruit pies speaks to our collective mythological childhoods in grandma's kitchen.

Fruit pies follow a general rule of thumb and also allow for some experimentation with sweeteners, herbs, and mixtures of fruit. They best exemplify the concept that if it tastes good in the bowl, it will taste good in the crust. They are a true celebration of the seasons and fresh food.

Working with Fruit in Season

Any fruit pie is improved when you can use fruit at the peak of its flavor. This is what "in season" means. We haven't tasted the real flavor of food until we have eaten it at this moment. Technology and travel have allowed us to eat any food at any moment, but this possibility does not mean we are eating the best food. Once you turn your brain a bit to think more seasonally, you begin to shudder at the thought of a tomato in February or a peach in November.

The best way to find out what is in season where you live is to go to a place where food is grown and speak to people who grow it. The real key to that question is the farmer's market. Go there and buy with impunity. And begin to really think about food and the weather. What food is growing when it's really hot out? What seems sturdier and more capable of growing as the frost approaches? If you can't really wrap your brain around that kind of situation, then you should just talk to a farmer. They know.

Selecting Fruit

Fruit costs a lot and should cost a lot of money. It requires a lot of labor to harvest, and we should be willing to pay for that.

Fruit continues to ripen off the vine or tree, gaining more flavor every day. Then it rots. Fruit will gain more flavor every day it is on the vine or tree. When you buy fruit, consider how long it has traveled to reach its point in your hand. If you buy from farmers' markets, it is completely possible it was picked the day before. If you purchase fruit at a giant supermarket, it's completely possible that it was on a plane, train, or boat for days. When that is the case, the fruit is picked really unripe and then allowed to somewhat ripen along its journey. There's something unappetizing about fruit that *commutes*. My one exception is lemons. I cannot fathom a world without lemons.

The more delicate fruits, such as raspberries, prefer to be stored in a single layer on kitchen towels at room temperature. Cover the fruit to keep away fruit flies. This is ideal for most fruit; then they don't crush each other. Even the hardier affairs like cherries, peaches, and plums like this kind of storage. It cuts down on bruising.

Leave fruit out at room temperature so it can continue to ripen. There is something wonderful about eating a tomato or peach that has never been refrigerated. The warmth of the sun is still apparent on it. It hasn't been sent to idle in cold storage; it's just been able to live out its life ripening naturally.

If fruit starts to turn, refrigerate or use it. I won't stand for a mailbox full of hate mail about kitchens overrun with fruit flies because common sense has been abandoned. Refrigeration is helpful in retarding ripening, thus enduring the life of the fruit.

The exception: Apples love refrigeration. Their crisp texture is important to their flavor.

Washing Fruit

When washing fruit, pick through for the moldy specimens. They can be detrimental to the life of the other fruit. Place the fruit in a colander and dip in a bowl of cool water repeatedly. Change the water if needed. You may also wipe the fruit with a clean towel. A lot of fruit is too delicate to be put under a stream of water. If you are able to get fruit from a good source, you don't have to worry as much about cleaning it.

Freezing Seasonal Fruit

You can also freeze fresh fruit for making pies later in the year. If you are in love with blueberry pie, then by all means freeze blueberries to pull out of the freezer in the dark of winter. Just make sure you use a container or freezer bag that won't completely succumb to freezer burn. You will thank yourself if you prepare your fruit before you freeze it. Months later when you pull out the fruit, you will be excited to see it's been picked through, peeled, and cut if need be. Just make sure it thaws a bit and drain off any water from it before you bake with it.

Pairing Food Seasonally

In the chill of late autumn, harvest time, the classic pies are pumpkin, sweet potato, pecan, and mincemeat. How incongruous would it be to serve blueberry pie at this time of year? Or strawberry rhubarb?

A cardinal rule of pairing food seasonally: Things that grow together work together. The world can make sense at times. Like grows with like. Trust the season for offering what works well together in flavor.

Another rule: Think of weather and colors for food. When I think of late autumn, I think of leaves changing, chills, and building fires. The colors are all burnt orange, deep red, and rich caramel brown, and the food is too. Pumpkin, apples, potatoes, sweet potatoes...

The hot, hot summer months coax the most flavor from peaches and blueberries with the long days and brutal sun, and early fall delivers plentiful apples. When you taste the flavor of food at its peak, you won't want to eat the stuff shipped from other hemispheres in the off-season. It's just not the same.

Bake Fresh

Nothing exemplifies the importance of seasonal pairings more than making fruit pies. If you use subpar fruit, your pie has no flavor. The sugar ends up doing most of the work. Subpar fruit has no flavor and hasn't been allowed to ripen. Commercial canned fruit rose to popularity in the mid-twentieth century, and its indefinite shelf life has skewed some palates. Some people don't even know what real peaches are supposed to taste like, but we know what they taste and look like from a can. Canned fruit is just the ghost of fruit covered in viscous, sugary syrup.

Sugar, Sugar

Neither I nor my pies are about sweetness. Know this so you can adapt the recipes for your taste. Sugar helps to bring out the flavor of the fruit, as does salt to a certain extent, until the amount overwhelms the fruit and makes the pie overly sweet.

Following Recipes

I generally follow a recipe as written the first time I make a dish and then make notes when I taste it to adjust it to my tastes. I suggest you do the same. It's good practice. Your cookbooks have wide margins for a reason.

- -

How much sugar do I add to fruit filling?

For fruit pies the general rule of thumb is if it tastes good in the bowl, it will taste good in the pie. There is no fixed flavor or ingredient proportion to the fruit you are using, so taste the filling mixture and adjust the ingredients as necessary.

- -

Rhubarb Pie

Crust

Basic Pie Crust (page 18), chilled

Filling

3 pounds (1.3 kg) rhubarb,
cut into ¼-inch (6 mm) pieces
on a slight bias

½ cup (100 g) granulated sugar

½ cup (115 g) packed brown sugar

1 teaspoon kosher salt

good grating of fresh nutmeg
(about 25 to 30 grates)

2 tablespoons (16 g) all-purpose flour

zest and juice of 1 lemon

20 to 30 chiffonade of fresh mint leaves

Wash

1 whole egg, beaten, or 3 tablespoons
(45 ml) heavy cream or whole milk

3 tablespoons (45 g) raw sugar

Spring is a tease. It warms up long before anything comes from the ground, leaving me impatient. And then rhubarb comes. Rhubarb is a declaration of the start of the growing season. Technically rhubarb is a vegetable, but it is used as a fruit. Its stalk is ideally tender and garnet in color. Seek tender, thin red stalks. Rhubarb that is big and green will be very tart.

Preheat the oven to 425°F (220°C, gas mark 7).

If you bake with really green, large rhubarb, bump up the sugar in the pie to counter its tartness. Try a mixture of white sugar and brown sugar with it.

Bottom Crust

Roll out your chilled bottom crust to no more than ⅛-inch (3 mm) thick. It should be about 16 inches (40 cm) in diameter. Place in your pie pan per the instructions in chapter 3. Trim the edges so there is no more than ¼ inch (6 mm) of overhang. Lift and crimp the overhang along the rim of the pie pan. Chill the bottom crust in the refrigerator or freezer.

Filling

Prepare the filling: Wash and wipe clean your stalks of rhubarb. Slice them on a slight bias no thicker than ⅓ inch (8 mm). Place in a medium-size bowl, toss with the ½ cup (100 g) of granulated sugar, and let sit for at least half an hour. This is called macerating the fruit. The sugar pulls some liquid from the fruit and softens it a bit, which is ideal for the stalky rhubarb. After at least 30 minutes, add the brown sugar, salt, nutmeg, flour, and lemon zest and juice. Make a chiffonade of your mint leaves by rolling the bunch into a tight pile and slicing into thin ribbons.

Smell the mixture—a little mist of mint, some lemon, the nuttiness of nutmeg. If you can smell it you can taste it. Pull the rhubarb out of the bowl and place in your chilled or frozen rolled-out crust and top with a lattice crust. Add any juice from your fruit as long as it not more than ¼ cup (60 ml).

Pull out your top crust and roll out for a lattice top. You should achieve the same thickness as the bottom crust. Cut the crust into lattice strips as instructed on pages 50–52.

Retrieve your chilled bottom crust.

Rhubarb is tart; it smacks our taste buds awake out of the long season of braised meat and cold-stored apples. It's like a young wine, before the earth and sun are warm and rich to lend heat to the food. Rhubarb pie pairs well with sweetened whipped cream or vanilla ice cream. You cannot change rhubarb, so if you desire something sweeter, move on. Appreciate it for what it is.

Wash

Whip up your egg or get your cream in a bowl. Gently wash the top of the crust with a pastry brush. It's okay if it gets on the fruit. This wash does not affect the flavor of the filling; it just adds a great crunch and depth to the top crust. Sprinkle evenly with the raw sugar.

Bake

Create your aluminum foil barrier and place atop the pie. You want it to shield the crust from the heat, but you do not want to press the foil down upon the crust because it will stick to it and come up with the foil when you remove it.

Bake the pie at 425°F (220°C, gas mark 7) for 30 minutes. Then carefully remove the foil, rotate the pie 180 degrees, and lower your oven to 350°F (180°C, gas mark 4) for the following 30 minutes. The pie is done when you can see that the bottom crust is golden, about an hour total.

Pull the pie and let it cool for at least 2 hours.

Yield: 1 pie (8 servings)

Strawberry Rhubarb Pie

Crust

Basic Pie Crust (or use shortening or lard), page 18, chilled

Filling

1 ½ pounds (680 g) rhubarb

1 ½ pounds (680 g) strawberries

½ cup (100 g) granulated sugar

1 teaspoon kosher salt

zest and juice of 1 lemon

¼ cup (60 g) packed brown sugar

2 tablespoons (16 g) thickener of your choice (see page 15)

Wash

1 whole egg, beaten, or 3 tablespoons (45 ml) heavy cream or whole milk

3 tablespoons (45 g) raw sugar

As the days become hotter and longer, strawberries gain more flavor. They are a fantastic accompaniment to rhubarb. After making loads of apple pies I finally tackled strawberry rhubarb pie without an inkling of its meaning for many. This pie breaks a lot of hearts and brings strangers into the fold to become friends. It is a powerful, powerful pie.

Strawberry rhubarb pie is delicious and incredibly juicy. You want to macerate the rhubarb and strawberries for at least 30 minutes before putting it in the pie plate and baking. Lift the fruit out of the juice with your hands or a slotted spoon. Do not add that juice to the pie. I know it sounds counterintuitive. Your pie will create enough liquid on its own as it bakes.

Instead, reserve that liquid and add it to seltzer or tonic water, or braise something in it or freeze it to pull out in some midwinter dark moment of desperation for something different.

Preheat the oven to 425°F (220°C, gas mark 7).

Bottom Crust

Roll out your chilled bottom crust to no more than ⅛-inch (3 mm) thick. It should be about 15 inches (38 cm) in diameter. Place in your pie pan per the instructions in chapter 3. Trim the edges so there is no more than ¼ inch (6 mm) of overhang. Lift and crimp the overhang along the rim of the pie pan. Chill the bottom crust in the refrigerator or freezer.

Filling

Prepare your filling. Wash and wipe dry your rhubarb stalks. Cut on a slight angle no more than ⅓ inch (8 mm) thick. Hull your strawberries. Cut them in half or leave them whole if they are small. Place the rhubarb and strawberries in a bowl and add the granulated sugar and the teaspoon of salt. Let sit for at least half an hour. This is called macerating the fruit, and in this case it pulls out a lot of liquid and gets the rhubarb tender. This is a cripplingly juicy pie.

After 30 minutes pull the fruit out of the bowl with your hands and place in another bowl. Add the lemon zest and juice, brown sugar, and thickener. Save the macerated juice for a drink, something with soda water, lime, and possibly vodka. Or freeze it to discover during a dark winter month. Just do not put it in this pie.

Lattice Crust

Roll out your second crust for lattice. You should achieve the same thickness as the bottom crust. Cut the crust into lattice strips as instructed on pages 50–52.

Wash

Whip up your egg or get your cream in a bowl. Gently wash the top of the crust with a pastry brush. It's okay if it gets on the fruit. This wash does not affect the flavor of the filling. It just adds a great crunch and depth to the top crust. Sprinkle evenly with the raw sugar.

Bake

Create your aluminum foil barrier and place it atop the pie. You want it to shield the crust from the heat, but you do not want to press the foil down upon the crust because it will stick to it and come up with the foil when you remove it.

Bake the pie at 425°F (220°C, gas mark 7) for 30 minutes. Then carefully remove the foil, rotate the pie 180 degrees, and lower the oven to 350°F (180°C, gas mark 4) for the following 30 minutes. The pie is done when you can see that the bottom crust is golden, about an hour total.

This pie must rest for at least 3 hours before it is served.

Yield: 1 pie (8 servings)

Raspberry Pie
with Shortening Crust

Crust

Basic Pie Crust (substitute shortening for the butter), page 18, chilled

Filling

5 cups (625 g) raspberries

1 cup (200 g) granulated sugar

1 teaspoon (6 g) kosher salt

zest and juice of 1 lemon

2 tablespoons (16 g) thickener of your choice (see page 15)

Wash

1 whole egg, beaten, or 3 tablespoons (45 ml) heavy cream or whole milk

3 tablespoons (45 g) raw sugar

This recipe is only made with a shortening crust. Butter overwhelms the raspberries. Shortening offers the function of fat with the flavor of butter, so a lovely lilting fruit like the raspberry can shine.

The day I figured out I could make great pie crust with just butter and no shortening, I became a little cocky. I no longer had to depend on the crutch of shortening for pie, and it was one less thing my pantry needed. And I kept on this haughty path until my friend Annaliese Griffin steered me differently. She told me about this. Her grandmother Olive Griffin's raspberry pie recipe had been handed down from great aunt Marion. The original recipe is old school, calling for just raspberries, tapioca, and sugar. I've tweaked it just a bit, but really nothing needs to change that much for this gem.

RIDICULOUSLY DELICATE RASPBERRIES

Preheat the oven to 425°F (220°C, gas mark 7).

Bottom Crust

Roll out your chilled bottom crust to ⅛-inch (3 mm) thick. It should be about 13 inches (33 cm) in diameter. Place in your pie pan per the instructions in chapter 3. Trim the edges so there is no more than ¼ inch (6 mm) of overhang. Lift and crimp the overhang along the rim of the pie pan. Chill the bottom crust in the refrigerator or freezer.

Filling and Top Crust

Pick through the raspberries for any moldy ones. Put in a bowl with the sugar, salt, lemon zest and juice, and thickener. Pull out your top crust and roll it out for a lattice top. You should achieve the same thickness as the bottom crust. Cut the crust into lattice strips as instructed on pages 50–52.

Wash

Whip up your egg or get your cream in a bowl. Gently wash the top of the crust with a pastry brush. It's okay if it gets on the fruit. This wash does not affect the flavor of the filling; it just adds a great crunch and depth to the top crust. Sprinkle evenly with the raw sugar. Create your aluminum foil barrier and place atop the pie. You want it to shield the crust from the heat, but you do not want to press the foil down upon the crust because it will stick to it and come up with the foil when you remove it.

Bake

Bake the pie at 425°F (220°C, gas mark 7) for 30 minutes. Then carefully remove the foil, rotate the pie 180 degrees, and lower your oven to 350°F (180°C, gas mark 4) for the following 30 minutes. The pie is done when you can see that the bottom crust is golden, about an hour total.

Pull and let sit for 2 hours.

Yield: 1 pie (8 servings)

Cherry Pie

Crust

Basic Pie Crust (page 18), chilled

Filling

2 pounds (910 g) cherries,
  any combination of types, pitted

⅓ cup (75 g) packed brown sugar

⅓ cup (67 g) granulated sugar

  zest and juice of 2 small limes or 1 large

  juice of 1 lemon

1 teaspoon (6 g) kosher salt

2 tablespoons (16 g) thickener
  of your choice (see page 15)

Wash

1 whole egg, beaten, or 3 tablespoons
  (45 ml) heavy cream or whole milk

3 tablespoons (45 g) raw sugar

Cherries: So many kinds, some fleeting, some stable. They are amazing, meaty creatures that deliver a lot of flavor. Sour cherries are a favorite of mine; they have a ghostly translucence, and their flavor is incredible. I like it when nature throws us a curveball and makes something seemingly innocent sour or spicy. It keeps us on our toes.

Cherries can handle a lot of flavor, and they give a lot. Adding lime adds a deeper acidic flavor than lemon, more suited to the meat of the cherry. Along with that I use a combination of white and brown sugar.

Preheat the oven to 425°F (220°C, gas mark 7).

Bottom Crust

Roll out your chilled bottom crust to ⅛-inch (3 mm) thick and about 15 inches (38 cm) in diameter. Place in your pie pan per the instructions in chapter 3. Trim the edges so there is no more than ¼ inch (6 mm) of overhang. Lift and crimp the overhang along the rim of the pie pan. Chill the bottom crust in the refrigerator or freezer.

Filling

Prepare your filling. Pop and stem all the cherries and place in a bowl. Add the sugar, salt, lime zest and juice, lemon juice, and thickener. You don't have to macerate the cherries; they hold their shape really well after baking. Cherries are more about flesh than juice.

Lattice Crust

Pull out your top crust and roll out for a lattice top. You should achieve the same thickness as the bottom crust. Cut the crust into lattice strips as instructed on page 50.

Get your bottom crust out and put your filling in it. Now construct your lattice crust according to the instructions on pages 50–52.

Wash

Whip up your egg or get your cream in a bowl. Gently wash the top of the crust with a pastry brush. It's okay if it gets on the fruit. This wash does not affect the flavor of the filling; it just adds a great crunch and depth to the top crust. Sprinkle evenly with the raw sugar.

Bake

Create your aluminum foil barrier and place it atop the pie. You want it to shield the crust from the heat, but you do not want to press the foil down upon the crust because it will stick to it and come up with the foil when you remove it.

Bake the pie at 425°F (220°C, gas mark 7) for 30 minutes. Then carefully remove the foil, rotate the pie 180 degrees, and lower your oven to 350°F (180°C, gas mark 4) for the following 30 minutes. The pie is done when you can see that the bottom crust is golden, about an hour total.

Pull the pie and let it cool for at least 2 hours.

Yield: 1 pie (8 servings)

SOUR CHERRIES

RAINIER CHERRIES

Blueberry Pie

Crust

Basic Pie Crust (page 18), chilled

Filling

6 cups (870 g) blueberries

¾ cup (150 g) granulated sugar

zest and juice of 1 lemon

2 tablespoons (16 g) thickener
of your choice (see page 15)

⅛ teaspoon freshly grated nutmeg
(about 15 grates)

Wash

1 whole egg, beaten, or 3 tablespoons
(45 ml) heavy cream or whole milk

3 tablespoons (45 g) raw sugar

- - - - - - - - - - - - - - - - - - -

My friend Eben Burr adds a handful of
dried blueberries in place of the thickener.
It's a brilliant move. The dried berries rehy-
drate with the juice of the fresh ones. The
tiniest blueberries have the most flavor.
They may just be the size of a pinhead,
but really you haven't eaten a blueberry
until you've had a tiny wild one.

- - - - - - - - - - - - - - - - - - -

Like a lot of other fruits that love the heat, blueberries come up with a scent but a light flavor
and then move on to become more intense as
the sun becomes hotter. If you're lucky, you can
find blueberries on the bush in season that are
the size of a pinhead. Barring that, go for any
blueberries you find in farmer's markets in late
summer. The heat of these months and the
length of the days intensify the flavor of fruit.

Blueberry pie is incredibly juicy. Allow at least 4 hours
after baking for your pie to set before you serve it.

Preheat the oven to 425°F (220°C, gas mark 7).

Bottom Crust

Roll out your chilled bottom crust to ⅛-inch (3 mm)
thick. It should be about 15 inches (38 cm) in diameter.
Place in your pie pan per the instructions in the
chapter 3. Trim the edges so there is no more than
¼ inch (6 mm) of overhang. Lift and crimp the overhang along the rim of the pie pan. Chill the bottom
crust in the refrigerator or freezer.

Filling

Pick through your blueberries for any stems, duds, or
green ones and discard them. Put the cleaned berries
in a bowl with the sugar, lemon zest and juice, thickener, and nutmeg. The nutmeg adds a little hint of
warmth to the flavor of the pie at the very end.

Lattice Crust

Pull out your top crust and roll out for a lattice top. You should achieve the same thickness as the bottom crust. Cut the crust into lattice strips as instructed on page 50.

Put your blueberry filling in the pie plate. Now construct your lattice crust according to the instructions on pages 50–52.

Wash

Whip up your egg or get your cream in a bowl. Gently wash the top of the crust with a pastry brush. It's okay if it gets on the fruit. This wash does not affect the flavor of the filling; it just adds a great crunch and depth to the top crust. Sprinkle evenly with the raw sugar.

Granulated sugar is great for blueberries because it's a less invasive sweetener, as opposed to brown sugar.

Bake

Create your aluminum foil barrier and place atop the pie. You want it to shield the crust from the heat, but you do not want to press the foil down upon the crust because it will stick to it and come up with the foil when you remove it.

Bake the pie at 425°F (220°C, gas mark 7) for 30 minutes. Then carefully remove the foil, rotate the pie 180 degrees, and lower your oven to 350°F (180°C, gas mark 4) for the following 30 minutes. The pie is done when you can see that the bottom crust is golden, about an hour total.

Pull the pie and let it cool for at least 3 hours. Blueberry pie is really, really juicy.

Yield: 1 pie (8 servings)

Peach Pie

Peaches hit at the height of summer, like corn and tomatoes. Grab them, any of them, and make a pie.

Peaches make gorgeous pies, mix well with other summer fruits, and offer what only a peach can offer: that unmistakable mixture of flesh, juice, and give to each bite. Peaches pair well with herbs. I recommend basil, thyme, lemon thyme, mint, or chervil for this pie.

Preheat the oven to 425°F (220°C, gas mark 7).

Bottom Crust

Roll out your chilled bottom crust to ⅛-inch (3 mm) thick. It should be about 15 inches (38 cm) in diameter. Place in your pie pan per the instructions in the chapter 3. Trim the edges so there is no more than ¼ inch (6 mm) of overhang. Lift and crimp the overhang along the rim of the pie pan. Chill the bottom crust in the refrigerator or freezer.

Filling

Peel your peaches and cut in half along the core. Twist the halves and pull apart. Pick the pit out with a knife. Cut the peaches into ¼-inch (6 mm) wedges and put in a bowl with the sugar, salt, citrus zest and juice, thickener, and herb if you choose to use one. Slightly mix the ingredients. Peaches do not have to sit and macerate.

Lattice Crust

Pull out your top crust and roll out for a lattice top. You should achieve the same thickness as the bottom crust. Cut the crust into lattice strips as instructed on page 50.

Get your chilled bottom crust and put your filling in it. Now construct your lattice crust according to the instructions on pages 50–52.

Crust

Basic Pie Crust (page 18), chilled

Filling

2 pounds (910 g) ripe peaches, any variety

½ cup (115 g) packed light brown sugar

1 teaspoon kosher salt

zest and juice of 1 lemon

2 tablespoons (16 g) thickener of your choice (see page 15)

3 tablespoons (9 g) picked herb (optional)

Wash

1 whole egg, beaten, or 3 tablespoons (45 ml) heavy cream or whole milk

3 tablespoons (45 g) raw sugar

Wash

Whip up your egg or get your cream in a bowl. Gently wash the top of the crust with a pastry brush. It's okay if it gets on the fruit. This wash does not affect the flavor of the filling; it just adds a great crunch and depth to the top crust. Sprinkle evenly with the raw sugar.

Bake

Create an aluminum foil barrier atop the pie. It will shield the crust from the heat. Do not press the foil down on the crust; it will stick and come up with the foil when you remove it.

Bake the pie at 425°F (220°C, gas mark 7) for 30 minutes. Carefully remove the foil, rotate the pie 180 degrees, and lower your oven to 350°F (180°C, gas mark 4) for 30 minutes. The pie is done when the bottom crust is golden, about an hour .

Pull the pie and let it cool for at least 2 hours.

Yield: 1 pie (8 servings)

Peach Blueberry Pie

Peach blueberry pie should be as classic as strawberry rhubarb pie. It is a beautiful combination both visually and flavor-wise.

Preheat the oven to 425°F (220°C, gas mark 7).

Bottom Crust

Roll out your chilled bottom crust to ⅛-inch (3 mm) thick and about 15 inches (38 cm) in diameter. Place in your pie pan per the instructions in chapter 3. Trim the edges so there is no more than ¼ inch (6 mm) of overhang. Lift and crimp the overhang along the rim of the pie pan. Chill the bottom crust in the refrigerator or freezer.

Filling

Sort through your blueberries for any stems or duds. Peel your peaches, cut in half along the pit, and twist and separate. Cut into ¼-inch (6 mm) wedges and put in a bowl with the blueberries, sugar, salt, lemon zest and juice, thickener, and nutmeg.

Lattice Crust

Roll your top crust out for a lattice top. You should achieve the same thickness as the bottom crust. Cut the crust into lattice strips as instructed on page 50.

Get your chilled bottom crust. Put the contents of the bowl in the pie plate and construct the lattice as instructed on pages 50–52.

Wash

Whip up your egg or get your cream in a bowl. Gently wash the top of the crust with a pastry brush. It's okay if it gets on the fruit. This wash does not affect the flavor of the filling; it just adds a great crunch and depth to the top crust. Sprinkle evenly with the raw sugar.

Crust

Basic Pie Crust (page 18), chilled

Filling

- 1 pound (455 g) blueberries
- 1 pound (455 g) peaches
- ¾ cup (150 g) granulated sugar
- 1 teaspoon kosher salt
- zest and juice of 1 lemon
- 2 tablespoons (16 g) thickener of your choice (see page 15)
- ⅛ teaspoon fresh nutmeg (about 15 grates)

Bake

Create your aluminum foil barrier and place atop the pie. You want it to shield the crust from the heat, but you do not want to press the foil down upon the crust because it will stick to it and come up with the foil when you remove it.

Bake the pie at 425°F (220°C, gas mark 7) for 30 minutes. Then carefully remove the foil, rotate the pie 180 degrees, and lower your oven to 350°F (180°C, gas mark 4) for the following 30 minutes. The pie is done when you can see that the bottom crust is golden, about an hour total.

Pull the pie and let it cool for at least 4 hours.

Yield: 1 pie (8 servings)

Apricot Tomatillo Pie

Crust

Basic Pie Crust (page 18), chilled

Filling

1 pound (300 g) overripened tomatillos

1 pound (300 g) ripe apricots

¾ cup (170 g) packed brown sugar (light or dark)

1 teaspoon (6 g) kosher salt

heaping ⅛ teaspoon grated nutmeg (about 25 grates)

zest of 1 lemon

zest and juice of 1 lime

2 tablespoons (16 g) thickener of your choice (see page 15)

Wash

1 whole egg, beaten, or 3 tablespoons (45 ml) heavy cream or whole milk

3 tablespoons (45 g) raw sugar

Tomatillos are a fruit, but they are often used in savory dishes like salsa. Overripened, they become paler, almost yellow from their intense ripe green, and gain a lovely sweetness that also occurs with other vegetables, such as parsnips.

Ladleah Dunn, an amazing, resourceful lady who cooks, plants, and maintains gardens, cajoled me to use a bounty of overripe tomatillos one summer for a dessert. This pie is what I dreamed up.

Preheat the oven to 425°F (220°C, gas mark 7).

Bottom Crust

Roll out 1 chilled crust to no more than ⅛-inch (3 mm) thick and about 16 inches (40.6 cm) in diameter. Place in your pie pan per the instructions in chapter 3. Trim the edges so there is no more than ¼ inch (6 mm) of overhang. Lift and crimp the overhang along the rim of the pie pan. Place the bottom crust in the refrigerator or freezer while you prepare the filling.

Filling

Place the tomatillos in a bowl of cool water and then peel off their papery husks. Cut them in half, down the stem, and then cut them into ¼-inch (6 mm) wedges. If the tomatillo is longer than 2 inches (5.1 cm), then cut the wedge in half. Halve and pit the apricots. Cut apricots into ¼-inch (6 mm) wedges. Toss the fruit in a large bowl with the sugar, salt, nutmeg, citrus zest, and juice.

If the fruit is not quite ripe, it's a good idea to let the sugar macerate it a bit. Let the filling mixture sit for no longer than half an hour.

Lattice Crust

Roll out the chilled top crust to the same thickness as the bottom crust. Cut the crust into lattice strips as shown in the tutorial on page 50.

Remove the chilled bottom crust from the refrigerator or freezer. Stir 2 tablespoons (16 g) of thickener into the filling, and then pour the filling into the bottom pie crust (b). Tomatillos and apricots benefit from a little liquid from their maceration, so pour up to ½ cup (120 ml) of the liquid to the pie.

Build your lattice crust (see pages 50–52).

Wash

Whip up an egg or pour cream or milk into a small bowl. Gently wash the top of the crust with a pastry brush. It's okay if it gets on the fruit. This wash does not affect the flavor of the filling; it just adds a great crunch and depth to the top crust. Sprinkle the raw sugar evenly on top.

Bake

Shape a round aluminum foil barrier that covers the top crust completely. Perch it atop the pie. It must shield the crust from the heat, but do not press the foil down on the crust. (This prevents the unbaked crust from sticking to the foil when you remove it.)

Bake the pie at 425°F (220°C, gas mark 7) for 30 minutes. Carefully remove the foil, rotate the pie 180 degrees in the oven, and reduce the oven temperature to 350°F (180°C, gas mark 4). Bake for another 30 minutes. The pie is done when you can see that the bottom crust is golden, about an hour total.

Remove the pie from the oven and let it cool for at least 2 hours. Serve.

Yield: 1 pie (8 servings)

Apple Pie

Crust

Double Cheddar Cheese Crust
(pages 33-35)

Filling

zest of 1 lemon and juice of 2

2 pounds (910 g) apples,
about 8 medium size

½ cup (115 g) packed brown sugar

¼ cup (50 g) granulated sugar

1 teaspoon kosher salt

1 knob raw ginger, about 1 inch (2.5 cm),
peeled

¼ teaspoon freshly grated nutmeg
(about 30 grates)

⅛ teaspoon freshly grated cinnamon stick
(about 20 grates)

¼ teaspoon ground mace

1 teaspoon vanilla extract

2 tablespoons (16 g) thickener
of your choice (see page 15)

optional: shot of maple syrup
or whiskey

Wash

1 whole egg, beaten, or 3 tablespoons
(45 ml) heavy cream or whole milk

Apple pie hits the kitchen when there are no other fruits in sight. There are so many kinds of apples it can boggle the mind, and sheer abundance of varieties of apples and their affordable price will keep you busy through the dark autumn months and bleak winter.

Tart and crisp apples stand up to a lot of flavor in a pie filling. Macoun, Braeburn, Crispin, Mutsu, Jonagold, Northern Spy, Ginger Gold, Fuji—there are so many kinds that cycle through the long season. Try buying apples on a whim according to name; Cripps Pink, aka Pink Ladies, anyone? A small apple called Newtown Pippin is the apple that allegedly inspired Sir Isaac Newton's discovery of the theory of gravity. How often does a trip to the apple stand invoke a historical science fact? Not nearly enough.

Apples have a lot of naturally acting pectin, which reduces the amount of liquid in the filling, so this is the time to use the solid top crust, albeit with steam slits. Use a pie bird. When there is a pie bird in the crust, its little ceramic beak sticks out the top, piping steam out.

Apple pie is a bridge between Cheddar cheese and vanilla ice cream. How could all of these things go together in such a delicious manner? It's such a tremendous range of flavor that really opens the mind to accept something sweet and something savory together in one bite. The richness of the cheese works with the creaminess of the ice cream, the crispness of the pie crust, and the give of the tart apples. It all works together; it's harmonious.

I like to add Cheddar cheese directly to the pie crust. The incorporation of the cheese to the baked pie crust enriches the flavor and sharpness of the

cheese and the depth of the apples. The smell when it comes out of the oven is overwhelming, in a good way. Like a pile of dry leaves on fire; it's a scent you can't get enough of.

Preheat the oven to 425°F (220°C, gas mark 7).

Bottom Crust

Roll out your chilled bottom crust to ⅛-inch (3 mm) thick and about 13 inches (33 cm) in diameter. Place in your pie pan per the instructions in chapter 3. Trim the edges so there is no more than ¼ inch (6 mm) of overhang. Lift and crimp the overhang along the rim of the pie pan. Chill the bottom crust in the refrigerator or freezer.

Filling

Juice 1 lemon and put it in a bowl with ½ cup (120 ml) water. Peel the apples and cut into slices no thicker than ¼ inch (6 mm). Put in the lemon juice water and give it all a toss so all of the surface areas of the apple slices come in contact with the lemon water. This eliminates the oxidation of the apples; that is, they won't turn brown. This step can be skipped if you are immediately baking the pie, but if you are preparing the apples earlier than 30 minutes before baking, this step is good to do. Drain the lemon juice and add the brown and white sugars, salt, ginger, lemon zest and juice, nutmeg, cinnamon, mace, vanilla, and thickener.

Pull your chilled bottom crust out of the refrigerator. If using a pie bird, place it, beak up, in the middle of the bottom crust with the apples around the bird. If not using a pie bird put the filling in the crust.

Top Crust

Pull the chilled crust disk from the refrigerator and roll out as you did the bottom crust. Place the filled pie pan adjacent to the top crust and treat it the same way, quickly flip it in half, and lift on top of the pie. Lift the other half over the pie. If there is a pie bird, just punch its beak through the top crust to vent. Lift the edges of the top crust so it lies on top of the apples, as opposed to being stretched across. Trim the edges to be flush with the rim and pinch together. If the crust sticks to your fingertips, put your fingertips in your bench flour. If the crusts don't adhere to each other, wet your fingertips a bit.

Wash

Wash your crust and sprinkle it with 4 tablespoons of sugar. Cut slits in the top crust, piercing through it so steam can be released. Create your aluminum foil barrier and place atop the pie. You want it to shield the crust from the heat, but you do not want to press the foil down upon the crust because it will stick to it and come up with the foil when you remove it.

Bake

Bake the pie at 425°F (220°C, gas mark 7) for 30 minutes. Then carefully remove the foil, rotate the pie 180 degrees, and lower your oven to 350°F (180°C, gas mark 4) for the following 30 minutes. The pie is done when you can see that the bottom crust is golden, about an hour total.

Pull the pie and let it cool for at least an hour.

Yield: 1 pie (8 servings)

Deep Dish Dutch Apple Pie

Often our motivation in cooking is to replicate something that's gone missing from our lives. Greta Dana, from Williamsburg, Brooklyn, delivers this classic German recipe that she cracked the code on. She found this pie at a fancy Mexican restaurant in Austin, Texas. Once they took it off the menu, she figured out the recipe. This is a delicious behemoth of a pie.

Use a deep 9½-inch (24 cm) pie plate if possible.

Preheat the oven to 475°F (240°C, gas mark 9).

Bottom Crust

Roll out your chilled bottom crust to ⅛-inch (3 mm) thick. It should be about 13 inches (33 cm) in diameter. Place in your pie pan per the instructions in chapter 3. Trim the edges so there is no more than ¼ inch (6 mm) of overhang. Lift and crimp the overhang along the rim of the pie pan. Chill the bottom crust in the refrigerator or freezer.

Filling

In a large mixing bowl whisk together the sour cream and egg. Add the sugar, flour, salt, and vanilla. Mix. Add the sliced apples and toss to coat them in the sour cream mixture. Pull your chilled crust out, fill with the apple mixture, and top with walnut crumb topping.

Crumble Topping

Mix together the flour, brown sugar, cinnamon, and salt. Scatter the chopped nuts over the dry ingredients then cut the softened butter into ¼-inch (6 mm) chunks. Toss the butter in the bowl, and quickly incorporate into the rest of the ingredients, breaking the butter down a bit until it's all a delicious, crumbly mix.

Crust

Single Pie Crust (page 19), chilled

Filling

1¼ cups (290 g) sour cream, room temperature

1 egg, room temperature

½ cup (115 g) packed brown sugar

4 tablespoons (32 g) all-purpose flour

½ teaspoon kosher salt

1 teaspoon vanilla extract

12 cups (1.3 kg) apples, peeled, quartered, cored, and sliced thinly

Crumb Topping

2 cups (250 g) all-purpose flour

1 cup (225 g) packed brown sugar

1 cup (225 g) softened butter

1 cup (120 g) chopped walnuts (or other nuts)

1 teaspoon cinnamon

1 teaspoon salt

Bake

Bake for 10 minutes at 475°F (240°C, gas mark 9), then lower the oven to 350°F (180°C, gas mark 4). Continue to bake for another hour or until the crust and topping are golden.

Yield: 1 pie (8 servings)

You may also feel the pull to create tall fluting for the edges of your crust. When your crust is raw they look great, but when you bake your pie these edges break off, and if you're lucky, they catch on fire in the bottom of your oven. Trim your crust to ¼ inch (6 mm) beyond the edges of your pie plate.

Boiled Cider Pie

Crust

Single Pie Crust (page 19), chilled

Filling

1 cinnamon stick

1 star anise

1 teaspoon (12 g) whole coriander seed

1 dried ancho pepper

8 cups (2 L) apple cider

2 tablespoons (28 g) unsalted butter

4 eggs, room temperature

¾ cup (170 g) maple sugar
   or packed light brown sugar

½ teaspoon (6 g) kosher salt

Wash

1 egg white

Prebake tools

aluminum foil

baking beans

One autumn, in my search to put apple pie on the menu without it being "apple pie," I found the Shakers and their uses of boiled cider. Boiled cider is apple cider reduced down to almost a syrup. I like to use eight cups of cider (that's half a gallon), and boil it down to a scant cup. Boiled cider is incredibly versatile; you can add any sort of spice to it while it evaporates away. I like this use in a pie. I think it's also a great use of cider. While cider is a great autumnal treat, I can never drink a whole jug before it turns. Even if your cider is just beginning to turn, you can still simmer it off for this recipe.

Maple sugar is the product of boiling off maple syrup until it becomes sugar. It's like gold for baking, both in its beauty and cost. Making maple sugar is tricky work; it should cost a pretty penny. In lieu of maple sugar I use brown sugar, usually light brown sugar, but if dark is all you have, it will do.

Preheat the oven to 425°F (220°C, gas mark 7).

Bottom Crust

Roll out your chilled pie crust to ⅛-inch (3 mm) thick. It should be about 13 inches (33 cm) in diameter. Place in your pie pan per the instructions in chapter 3. Trim the edges so there is no more than ¼ inch (6 mm) of overhang. Lift and crimp the overhang along the rim of the pie pan. Prick the bottom and the sides of the crust with a regular fork to prevent bubbles. Try to not pierce through the crust. If you can, chill your crust in the freezer for at least 15 minutes. If not, chill it in the refrigerator for at least 20 minutes. It is important for the crust to be very cold and the fat to re-form and firm up.

Pull your pie plate out of the refrigerator and place your foil in it. It should sit flush with the plate, come up along the rim, and fold down to cover the edges. This foil protects the crust from overbrowning, but you do not want the foil pressed securely to the edges. Place your baking beans in the bottom and level them out. Put the crust in the oven.

Bake the crust for 20 minutes at 425°F (220°C, gas mark 7). Then pull out the crust, lower your oven to 350°F (180°C, gas mark 4), and carefully lift the aluminum foil by the edges off your crust with the beans in it. Put your crust back in the oven for 10 minutes. Pull and let cool a bit.

Filling

Put the whole cinnamon stick, star anise, coriander seed, and dried ancho pepper in a small saucepan over medium heat. As soon as they become fragrant, add the 8 cups (2 L) of apple cider and simmer it all until it reduces to just under a cup (60 ml). It can take a bit over an hour, depending on your range. The cider will become darker in color, a truly rich amber, and thicker. Add the 2 tablespoons (28 g) of butter and mix it in. Strain out the aromatics.

Crack 3 of the eggs and place in a medium mixing bowl. Separate the yolk from the white on the last egg, adding the yolk to the other eggs and putting the white in a clean, dry mixing bowl. Whisk together the eggs and egg yolk, then add the sugar and salt. Quickly whip the egg white to soft peaks, about 5 minutes.

Add the slightly cooled but still warm cider-butter syrup to the eggs and sugar in a slow, steady stream. If you add it too fast you will scramble the eggs. The mixture will be a little lighter in color. Then quickly whisk in the whipped egg white, just integrating it.

Bake

Pour the filling into the par-baked crust and put it in the oven for 40 minutes. Give the pie a little shake. If most of it jiggles, put it back in the oven.

Pull and let sit for at least an hour.

Yield: 1 pie (8 servings)

Blackberry Banana Pie with a Crumble Top

Crust

Single Pie Crust (page 19), chilled

Filling

4 cups (580 g) rinsed blackberries

3 ripe bananas, sliced ¼ inch (6 mm)

1 cup (200 g) granulated sugar

1 teaspoon (6 g) kosher salt

zest and juice of 1 lemon

5 tablespoons (9.5 g) quick-cooking tapioca granules

1 tablespoon vanilla extract

Topping

1 Crumble Topping (see page 31)

Kelly Geary, owner of Sweet Deliverance in Brooklyn, New York, cooks incredible food using local markets; creates inventive and award-winning jams and chutneys; and wrote a book about canning and preserving.

So she knows a thing or two about pie. When asked what motivated her to create this pie she said, "There were blackberries growing in my backyard and bananas on the counter."

Preheat the oven to 425°F (220°C, gas mark 7).

Bottom Crust

Roll out your chilled bottom crust to ⅛-inch (3 mm) thick, and about 13 inches (33 cm) in diameter. Place in your pie pan per the instructions in chapter 3. Trim the edges so there is no more than ¼ inch (6 mm) of overhang. Lift and crimp along the rim of the pie pan. Chill the bottom crust in the refrigerator or freezer.

Filling

Mix the blackberries and bananas together with the sugar, salt, lemon juice and zest, tapioca, and vanilla. Toss gently. Set aside and assemble your crumble.

Bake

Pull the chilled pie plate out and fill with the fruit filling. Put the crumble on top and put it in the oven. Bake at 425°F (220°C, gas mark 7) for 30 minutes and then reduce the temperature to 350°F (180°C, gas mark 4) for 30 minutes. You don't need an aluminum foil barrier for the crumble top, but keep an eye on it. Better safe than sorry. Pull after an hour and cool.

Yield: 1 pie (8 servings)

Mincemeat Pie

Mincemeat pie is a strange bird. Is it dessert or dinner, or just oddly addictive? The ingredients and cooking methods date back to the period when European crusaders returned from the Holy Land.

Mincemeat pies have it all—they use citrus, booze, and loads of spices, dried fruit, and fresh fruit. The introduction of all of these things must have been mind-blowing to the English. So overwhelming, they just put them all in one pie. They traditionally also used meat, but over time have evolved, or devolved, depending on your feelings, to lose the meat and concentrate on the fruit.

Mincemeat pie historically utilizes animal fat, usually beef suet, as the general fat in the mince portion. Over time, as the pie has become relegated to dessert status, people have switched to butter for the filling. If you do have access to beef suet, use it instead of butter or a combination of suet and butter. Let's eat the past!

Preheat the oven to 400°F (200°C, gas mark 6).

Bottom Crust

Roll out your chilled bottom crust to ⅛-inch (3 mm) thick. It should be about 15 inches (38 cm) in diameter. Place in your pie pan per the instructions in chapter 3. Trim the edges so there is no more than ¼ inch (6 mm) of overhang. Lift and crimp the overhang along the rim of the pie pan. Chill the bottom crust in the refrigerator or freezer.

Crust

Basic Pie Crust (page 18), chilled

Filling (this can be made days in advance)

6 apples, peeled and chopped, no larger than ½ inch (1 cm) (I like a combo of Granny Smith and Braeburn, Gravenstein, and/or Pink Ladies.)

¾ cup (110 g) dark raisins

¾ cup (110 g) other dried fruit—golden raisins, apricots, dried cherries, or cranberries

1 cup (120 g) chopped nuts (all walnuts, ¾ cup walnuts + ¼ cup black walnuts, or 1 cup [110 g] pecans)

1 cup (200 g) granulated sugar

½ cup (120 ml) fresh-squeezed orange or tangerine juice

¼ cup (60 ml) bourbon

½ stick (¼ cup) (56 g) unsalted butter

zest and juice of 1 lemon

zest of 1 orange

2 tablespoons (28 ml) cider vinegar

1 teaspoon kosher salt

1 teaspoon cinnamon stick (about 40 grates)

1 teaspoon grated nutmeg (about 40 grates)

¼ teaspoon freshly ground black pepper

1 teaspoon grated fresh ginger

¼ teaspoon ground cloves

Wash

1 whole egg, beaten, or 3 tablespoons (45 ml) heavy cream or whole milk

3 tablespoons (45 g) raw sugar

Filling

Place all of the filling ingredients together in a medium-size saucepan. Peel and core the apples and give a rough chop to the raisins and other dried fruit and nuts. You want everything to be about the same size. Mix the fruit and nuts in the saucepan and add the sugar, juice, bourbon, butter, lemon zest and juice, orange zest, cider vinegar, and salt. Mix everything well and grate the cinnamon, nutmeg, pepper, and ginger over the mince. Add the cloves. Heat over medium or medium high at a strong simmer until the ingredients break down and create a viscous, syrupy mince, about 30 minutes. This mixture needs to cool to at least room temperature. Feel free to refrigerate it. The earlier you make this, the more the flavor becomes cohesive, with fewer sharp edges.

Lattice Crust

Take your top crust and roll it out to ⅛-inch thick (3 mm) for a lattice top. Mincemeat is traditionally a lattice crust. Pour the chilled mince into the bottom crust, construct your lattice as instructed on pages 50–52, and put the pie in the oven. It bakes at 400°F (200°C, gas mark 6) for 30 minutes, and then your oven is reduced to 250°F (120°C, gas mark 2) for another 30 minutes. You do not have to use a foil lid to protect the top crust at these temperatures. 250°F (120°C, gas mark 2) does not really brown your crust.

But just in case, check your pie at 30 minutes and then after 15 to make sure the crust isn't getting too dark. I can't be certain how your oven functions.

Pull the pie and let cool for at least 2 hours.

Yield: 1 pie (8 servings)

This recipe comes from my friend Caitlin Horsmon, who makes the only mincemeat pie I have eaten and liked. She should be writing this book about pies, as she knew more about a lattice crust before I first contemplated using a wine bottle as a rolling pin. She made this mincemeat pie one holiday. Her house was bustling with food preparation, and she used her carport as a makeshift walk-in refrigerator for stocks, stuffings, and baked goods. Caitlin made two gorgeous pies, this mincemeat and a sweet potato pie, and she placed them out in the carport to cool. After half an hour we checked on them, only to find some critter had discovered them first. The lattice on the mincemeat was crushed a bit, and a swipe had been taken from the sweet potato. Caitlin, ever the even-keeled soul, just laughed it off and mended the pies. And no one was the wiser. Until now.

Mock Mincemeat Pie

Here is a variation on a theme using a mixture of apples and green tomatoes, once again from Caitlin Horsmon.

Salting food, pulls out a lot of its moisture. Unripened green tomatoes still have a lot of liquid. The first step is salting them for an hour, straining, and rinsing the salt off. Just be mindful of your salt use.

Preheat the oven to 400°F (200°C, gas mark 6).

Bottom Crust

Roll out your chilled bottom crust to ⅛-inch (3 mm) thick, about 15 inches (38 cm) in diameter. Place in your pie pan per the instructions in chapter 3. Trim the edges so there is no more than ¼ inch (6 mm) of overhang. Lift and crimp the overhang along the rim. Chill in the refrigerator or freezer.

Filling

Chop your green tomatoes to about ¼ inch (6 mm). Toss in a colander with 2 teaspoons of kosher salt. Let sit for at least an hour. Rinse them well, and put in your saucepan.

Peel and core your apples, rough chop the raisins, dried fruit, and nuts all to about the same size. Mix into the saucepan, add the suet or butter, sugar, juices, brandy, cider vinegar, orange and lemon zest, and 1 teaspoon salt. Mix well, grate the cinnamon, nutmeg, ginger, and black pepper over the mince, and add the cloves and allspice. Heat over medium or medium high. Simmer until the ingredients break down to a viscous, syrupy mince; about 30 minutes. Cool to at least room temperature. The earlier you make this, the more cohesive the flavor becomes.

Top Crust

Mincemeat is traditionally a lattice crust. Construct your lattice as instructed on page 50, and bake.

Green Tomato Mock Mince Crust

Basic Pie Crust (page 18), chilled

10 small green tomatoes, cored and chopped

2 teaspoons (12 g) koshwer salt

6 apples, peeled and roughly chopped (I like a combo of Granny Smith and Braeburn, Gravenstein, and/or Pink Ladies)

Salt chopped tomatoes and let stand 1 hour. Rinse well.

¾ cup raisins

¾ cup golden raisins, dried cherries, or dried cranberries

1 cup (120 g) chopped nuts (I like walnuts and pecans)

¾ cup (168 g) beef suet or a mixture of butter and suet, or just butter

1 ½ cups (340 g) packed brown sugar

1 cup (235 ml) fresh-squeezed orange or tangerine juice

¼ cup (60 ml) brandy or red wine

¼ cup (60 ml) cider vinegar

zest of a lemon

zest of an orange

juice of ½ lemon

1 teaspoon (6 g) salt

1 teaspoon (3 g) cinnamon

½ teaspoon (3 g) freshly ground nutmeg

¼ cup (24 g) candied ginger, chopped fine

½ teaspoon black pepper

¼ teaspoon ground cloves

¼ teaspoon allspice

Bake

Bake at 400°F (200°C, gas mark 6) for 30 minutes, and reduce the temperature to 250°F (120°C, gas mark ½) for 30 minutes. Check your pie at 30 minutes then after 15 to make sure the crust isn't getting too dark.

Pull the pie and cool for 2 hours.

Yield: 1 pie (8 servings)

Paltry Fruit Pie

Crust

Single Pie Crust (page 19), chilled

Filling

at least 1 cup (about 170 g) fruit
(I used nectarines)

3 eggs, room temperature

1 cup (235 ml) buttermilk,
room temperature

¼ cup (60 g) packed brown sugar

½ cup (100 g) granulated sugar

1 teaspoon (6 g) kosher salt

zest and juice of 1 lemon

Wash

1 egg white

Prebake tools

aluminum foil

baking beans

Sometimes the problem with a new recipe is that it necessitates an elaborate trip to the supermarket, where you find yourself buying a whole cart of ingredients for one recipe. One dish! I err on the side of "make do" (plus, I hate grocery shopping), and this pie is an example of this ethos.

One day I found myself with about six nectarines that were about one day away from going bad. They smelled incredible and made me realize how in the land of stone fruit, for me, peaches eclipsed the equally delicious apricots, plums, and nectarines. These nectarines were sweet with a lush flavor and texture, almost pillowy. They were lovely. I had six, and I wasn't going to just eat six nectarines in a day. But I could add them to a pie.

Buttermilk pie is a little one-note: It needs a little something, either in it or at the end. These nectarines could only improve the custard of a buttermilk pie. I don't make pies entirely of nectarines, apricots, or plums. I don't think their texture is conducive to an entire slice of pie. But just a layer of them in this custard is a different story. I cut the granulated sugar with some brown. I found an entire cup of granulated sugar veered toward an almost processed flavor, so I countered it with a little warmth in the brown sugar.

If you aren't in the habit of using buttermilk, please welcome it into your world. Traditionally buttermilk is the liquid left when cream is churned for butter. Commercially available buttermilk is milk with a lactic acid bacteria added to it, giving it a tangy flavor and richness almost more like crème fraîche than milk or cream. It keeps for a long time and is great to use for baking pies or cakes, dressings, marinades, and more.

It's a great horse to have in your stable, adding almost a savory element to your sweets.

Almost any handful of fruit you have around will work with this recipe; you just want to at least cover the bottom of the crust. Tropical fruits and citrus are not so friendly with this dairy recipe.

Bottom Crust

Roll out your chilled pie crust to ⅛-inch (3 mm) thick. It should be about 13 inches (33 cm) in diameter. Place in your pie pan per the instructions in chapter 3. Trim the edges so there is no more than ¼ inch (6 mm) of overhang. Lift and crimp the overhang along the rim of the pie pan. Prick the bottom and the sides of the crust with a regular fork to prevent bubbles. Try to not pierce through the crust. If you can, chill your crust in the freezer for at least 15 minutes. If not, chill it in the refrigerator for at least 20 minutes. It is important for the crust to be very cold and the fat to re-form and firm up.

Pull your pie plate out of the refrigerator and place your foil in it. It should sit flush with the plate, come up along the rim, and fold down to cover the edges. This foil protects the crust from overbrowning, but you do not want the foil pressed securely to the edges. Place your baking beans in the bottom and level them out. Put the crust in the oven.

Bake the crust for 20 minutes at 425°F (220°C, gas mark 7). Then pull out the crust, lower your oven to 350°F (180°C, gas mark 4), and carefully lift the aluminum foil by the edges off your crust with the beans in it. Put your crust back in the oven for 15 minutes. Pull and let cool a bit.

Filling

Prepare whatever fruit you have on hand. If it is a stone fruit, cut it in half along the pit, hold either half in either hand, and gently twist. Slice into ¼-inch (6 mm) wedges. If it is a peach, peel it before any of this. If you have cherries, pit and stem them, blueberries check for duds and stems, strawberries hull and slice. You get the idea. Whisk together the room-temperature eggs with the room-temperature buttermilk. Add the brown and granulated sugar, salt, and lemon zest and juice to the dairy and mix well. Not so it's fluffy and full of bubbles, but just so it's mixed. Put the fruit on the bottom of the cooled pie crust and pour the mixture over it.

Bake

Place in the 350°F (180°C, gas mark 4) oven for an hour. Check after 30 minutes and rotate the pie 180 degrees. Check the pie again after 15 minutes, the 45-minute mark, to see how it's baking. The pie is finished when just the center jiggles a bit. Pull and let set and cool for at least an hour.

Yield: 1 pie (8 servings)

Poached Pear and Pastry Cream with Concord Grapes and Vanilla Wafer Crust

Crust

Vanilla wafer crumb crust (page 28), chilled

Filling: Poached Pears

1 lemon

2 pounds (910 g) ripe pears

1 star anise

1 cinnamon stick

2 cups (475 ml) white wine or rosé

Pinch of kosher salt

1 bay leaf

½ cup (170 g) maple syrup

1 pint Concord grapes, whole, pitted, or strained

Pastry Cream

1¼ cups (295 ml) whole milk

1 bay leaf

1 teaspoon whole coriander seeds

1 teaspoon whole black peppercorns

¼ cup (31 g) cake flour

4 egg yolks

½ cup (100 g) granulated sugar

1½ teaspoon kosher salt

1 teaspoon vanilla extract

Poached pears are classy. Any time you cook fruit in booze, it's an unnecessary and decadent step in life. Take that step. It can take a bit for pears to ripen, especially if they are really hard at purchase. Leave them out at room temperature; if you refrigerate them they will never ripen. Recipes short on ingredients need intensity of flavor. So begin with ripe pears.

This is all a mild, creamy, dreamy pie, from the vanilla wafer crust through the fluffy pastry cream and easy pears. Concord grapes make sense with pears because they grow at the same time. Concord grapes taste like a cartoon of what a grape should taste like, and they have a deep, gorgeous purple color. They have seeds that are surrounded by a massive flavor packet. The skin and the seeds is where the flavor is. You can find seedless grapes, or you could painstakingly deseed the grapes. I suggest you live a life where consuming the seeds of Concord grapes is not the end, but the beginning.

Squeeze your lemon and put the juice in a bowl with about ½ cup (120 ml) water. Peel the pears and cut in half. Pull the stem off the pear and use a teaspoon to core it. If the pears are massive, cut them into quarters. Put the peeled pears in the lemon water. Try to preserve the shape of the pears; they are lovely and graceful.

In a medium saucepan over medium flame quickly toast the star anise and cinnamon stick until fragrant. Add the wine, salt, bay leaf, and maple syrup. Bring to a light boil so everything mixes together and then add the pears with the lemon water. Allow to poach until the pears can easily be pierced with a butter knife, about 30 minutes. Pull the pears out and allow to cool on a baking sheet. Crank the heat on the poaching liquid and reduce it to a syrup, about ¾ cup (175 ml). Add the grapes and allow them to get coated. Reserve.

Pastry Cream
Scald the milk with the bay leaf, coriander seeds, and black peppercorns over medium heat. Just as a film covers the top of the liquid and a few bubbles steam out, turn it off. Add the cake flour, whisking it. Keep cooking, a minute or three, so that the flour dissolves.

Separate the eggs, putting the yolks in a bowl. Add the sugar and whisk well, until the mixture turns a lemon yellow color. Add the milk-flour combination in a thin stream so the yolks don't scramble. Pour it all back into the saucepan and cook over medium-low heat, attending to it the entire time. It should thicken in under 10 minutes. The consistency should be between a custard and a pudding—solid but not lumpy.

Assemble
Spoon the pastry cream on the bottom of the vanilla crumb crust. Chill for at least 15 minutes so it firms up. Spiral the poached pears on top of the pastry cream in a pattern. Don't mash them in, just place them on top. Finish with the Concord grape sauce, salt, and vanilla.

Allow it to set up for 30 minutes, then serve.

Yield: 1 pie (8 servings)

CHAPTER 5

Nuts, Chocolate, and Other Decadent Staple Pies

With fewer supplies than you make breakfast with, it's possible to make a pie and they are wonderful examples of the versatility of the pantry. These pies are called staple pies. At the very least you just need eggs, sugar, and some kind of milk to make a pie, and any nuts or chocolate or different sweets you have on top of that are gravy. The days don't have to be short and cold to bust out a staple pie. Staple pies are glorious any time of the year, and are really quite affordable.

Nothing utilizes more common sense than the staple pie. It asks for little and delivers much, transforming the pantry into dessert. All hail!

Prebaked Crust

Most staple pies call for a prebaked crust. A prebaked, or blind-baked crust is used when the crust won't be done cooking in the time that the filling finishes baking. I also prebake crusts when eggs are the main component of the filling. I think they prefer a lower temperature than the crust necessitates to bake.

When you prebake a crust, you are baking it without any filling. In my best-laid pan I use the 9-inch (23 cm) glass pie plate, not the 9 ½-inch (24 cm) pie plate. The 9-inch (23 cm) plate is a bit more shallow, so I find it to be more forgiving for a blind bake. The big fear with a blind bake is that the sides of the pie crust will sag and fall during the bake. When you use a more shallow pie plate, it is more forgiving; the sides of the 9 ½-inch (24 cm) plate are quite steep compared to the 9-inch (23 cm). Enough to influence your blind bake if your crust is stretched a bit.

There are a few tricks to blind baking a crust. Put your rolled-out crust in your freezer so it really firms up to the shape of the pie plate.

Baking beans are handy to preserve the shape of your crust, the bottom, and the edges. You don't want to fill the pie with beans all the way up the sides. Then the beans will be too heavy and influence your bottom crust negatively. I just use a 1-pound (455 g) bag of dried beans.

When the crust is baked at 425°F (220°C, gas mark 7) it is setting, and the water percentage of whatever fat you used is beginning to steam out and create flakes. However the crust cannot be exposed in the oven at such a high temperature, and then a lower one, for such a long time and not be completely burned.

Pour the beans into the foil and make sure they are level. Put the pie in a preheated 425°F (220°C, gas mark 7) oven. After 15 minutes, carefully pull the crust out. Lift the ends of the foil up all around the edges so it doesn't nick the crust, and place to the side. Turn your oven down to 350°F (180°C, gas mark 4) and return the crust to the oven.

For a partially baked crust, pull the crust out after 10 minutes. It will be very light in color and still a bit raw to the eye. For a completely baked crust, allow the crust to bake for at least 20 minutes total at 350°F (180°C, gas mark 4). It should be golden brown and matte, not shiny with fat.

- -

Optional Egg White Wash

An egg white wash on your prebaked crust helps to seal any ny holes and give a sheen to the crust. Just make sure the crust has cooled a little, or the egg white will cook and become opaque. Whip the egg white a bit so it brushes on more evenly.

- -

1 Right before you bake the crust, lightly prick across the bottom of the crust with a fork. You don't want to pierce the crust, just lightly indent it. This helps with quelling the bubbles a crust can create.

2 Line your very chilled crust with aluminum foil. It should be flush with the crust, go up along the inside edges, and curve over the edges so they are not exposed. The foil's job is twofold: It holds the beans so they can safely be taken out of the crust and makes sure the crust doesn't brown too much.

Sweet Potato Pie
with Sesame Praline

Crust

Single Pie Crust (page 19), chilled

Filling

2 pounds (910 g) sweet potatoes
or 3 cups roasted and put through a sieve

2 large eggs, room temperature

¾ cup (175 ml) heavy cream,
room temperature

¾ cup (170 g) packed light brown sugar

1 teaspoon (6 g) kosher salt

⅛ teaspoon ground mace

⅛ teaspoon fresh nutmeg (about 15 grates)

⅛ teaspoon cinnamon

1½ tablespoons (12 g) fresh ginger,
zested across a grater

zest and juice of 1 lemon

shot of bourbon

Praline

6 tablespoons (84 g) unsalted butter

6 tablespoons (90 g) packed brown sugar

6 tablespoons (90 ml) heavy cream

2 teaspoons kosher salt

¾ cup (108 g) sesame seeds, toasted

Wash

1 egg white

Prebake tools

aluminum foil

baking beans

Sweet potato pie is the first pie that gave me the feeling of the transformative ability of cooking and knowledge. My sweet potato pies have evolved over the years, from lumpy masses with whiskey to this more flanlike approach with whiskey. You may substitute pumpkin for sweet potatoes in this pie as well.

As much as I believe it's important to make pies with fresh fruit, it is really important to make this pie with actual sweet potatoes. Canned sweet potatoes and canned pumpkin have a disconcerting texture, one thought up by men in suits over a three-martini lunch. It's tantamount to public school or hospital food, something capable of holding its shape in times of need and needlessness. A starch should never be so gelatinous.

Buy sweet potatoes. It's a simple thing to do, and they should be readily available and affordable. There are a few ways to prepare them, but if you have the time I implore you to roast them. It gives you the best texture and allows a rich flavor to develop, rather than just boiling them. When I roast them (and this includes pumpkin), I like to toss the potatoes with a few different things to add flavor. These flavors becomes nuanced, just hints instead of sledgehammers. Sweet potatoes get along well with allspice, cloves, cinnamon, nutmeg, bay leaves, coriander, and mace. Certainly you don't have to use each and every one of these spices, and it's preferable to use them in their whole seed form. The whole seeds are really flavorable (or leaves in the manner of the bay leaf) and impart a flavor. It's akin to marinating the potatoes.

Preheat the oven to 425°F (220°C, gas mark 7).

Bottom Crust

Roll out your chilled pie crust to ⅛-inch (3 mm) thick and about 15 inches (38 cm) in diameter. Place in your pie pan per the instructions in chapter 3. Trim the edges so there is no more than ¼ inch (6 mm) of overhang. Lift and crimp the overhang along the rim of the pie pan. Chill your crust in the freezer for at least 15 minutes or chill in the refrigerator for at least 20 minutes. It is important for the crust to be very cold and the fat to re-form and firm up.

Pull your pie plate out of the refrigerator and place your foil in it. It should sit flush with the plate, come up along the rim, and fold down to cover the edges. This foil

protects the crust from overbrowning, but do not press the foil to the edges. Place your baking beans in the bottom and level them out. Put the crust in the oven.

Bake the crust for 20 minutes at 425°F (220°C, gas mark 7). Then pull out the crust, lower your oven to 375°F (190°C, gas mark 5), and carefully lift the aluminum foil by the edges off your crust with the beans in it. Put your crust back in the oven for 15 minutes. Check at 7 minutes and turn it 180 degrees.

Check your crust. The edges may be a little darker than the rest, but it should be set and very light in color. The bottom is more than likely a little bit bubbly and looks shiny. Let it cook a bit more, 5 minutes at the most, if the bottom is more shiny than matte. Then take the crust out and let it rest for 10 minutes. Lower the oven to 350°F (180°C, gas mark 4).

Filling

Roast your sweet potatoes (as much as 3 days in advance). When the potatoes are still warm, slip them out of their sleeves and push through a medium-size colander. If you have a high-power blender or food processor, use that, but in lieu of said equipment, push the sweet potatoes through a colander with a wide wooden spoon. This is an essential step, because the texture informs the loveliness of this pie.

If you have a blender or a hand mixer, pull it out. If not, wield your strongest whisk and your dominant hand. Don't use the blender or hand mixer on the first step of ricing the potatoes; they don't have enough horsepower, and you'll just end up with a gluey mess. Mix together your eggs and cream until homogenized. Add the 3 cups of sieved potatoes and mix until it's all together. Add the sugar, salt, spices, and bourbon. Mix until smooth.

Bake

Pour your sweet potato mixture into your cooled, partially baked pie crust. Put it in the oven. At 30 minutes turn it 180 degrees. Check the pie at 45 or 50 minutes. This takes about an hour to cook. The best way to check it is to put a butter knife in the middle or give it a shake. If the knife comes out pretty clean, it is good. For the same measure, if it's only the very middle of the pie that is jiggly, the pie is done. Pull it and let set for at least an hour. See steps 6 and 7 to add cooled praline.

Yield: 1 pie (8 servings)

1 To make the praline, melt your unsalted butter in a medium saucepan over medium heat. Add the brown sugar when the butter begins to bubble and whisk them together. Watch your heat, you don't want this to burn, but you want the brown sugar to dissolve into the butter, to cook together.

2 Add the heavy cream in a steady stream, whisking the whole time.

3 Stop whisking and let the this bubble a bit to come together. It's done when it ceases to taste just like butter, sugar and heavy cream, it's still raw. It will taste like a creamy caramel, about 5 or 7 minutes.

4 Add the salt to finish and whisk. Finish with the sesame seeds.

5 Mix the sesame seeds in so everything is well dispersed.

6 It is very important to let this praline sit and cool a bit. If you pour on the pie hot it will spill over the sides. Pour the cooled praline over a cooled pie. Let it firm up a bit, about 30 minutes.

7 It should coat the entire top.

Walnut Maple Pie

Annaliese Griffin offers this pie that is a mash-up of French Canadian maple sugar pie and pecan pie.

Maple sugar is tricky to find, and can be prohibitively expensive. This pie cuts the difference and uses maple syrup—Grade B, not A, ends up being a more appropriate maple syrup for the rich flavor. Nuts, brown sugar and maple syrup work together really well, all they seem to be missing is a roaring fire.

Preheat the oven to 425°F (220°C, gas mark 7).

Bottom Crust

Roll out your chilled pie crust to ⅛-inch (3 mm) thick. It should be about 15 inches (38 cm) in diameter. Place in your pie pan per the instructions in chapter 3. Trim the edges so there is no more than ¼ inch (6 mm) of overhang. Lift and crimp the overhang along the rim of the pie pan. Chill the pie crust ideally in your freezer for at least 20 minutes, or 30 minutes in your refrigerator. It is really important for your crust to set again and the fat to refirm before you prebake.

Pull your pie plate out of the refrigerator and place your foil in it. It should sit flush with the plate, come up along the rim, and fold down to cover the edges. This foil protects the crust from overbrowning, but you do not want the foil pressed securely to the edges. Place your baking beans in the bottom and level them out. Put the crust in the oven. After 15 minutes carefully pull the foil and beans out of the crust and lower the temperature to 350°F (180°C, gas mark 4). Put the crust back in the oven for about 10 more minutes. Pull out of the oven and let cool for at least 15 minutes.

Crust

Single Pie Crust (page 19), chilled

Filling

- 2 cups (200 g) walnuts whole walnuts and large pieces preferably, toasted
- ½ cup (115 g) packed light brown sugar
- 2 large eggs, room temperature
- ½ cup (120 ml) heavy cream, room temperature
- 1 cup (340 g) pure maple syrup (as dark as you can find)
- 2 teaspoons (10 g) unsalted butter, melted
- ½ teaspoon kosher salt

Prebake tools

aluminum foil

baking beans

Filling

Arrange the nuts on the bottom of the par-baked crust in a spiral pattern.

Whisk the brown sugar and eggs together until pale and foamy, continue whisking, and add the cream, maple syrup, and salt. Whisk until smooth and creamy. Pour over the walnuts.

Bake at 350°F (180°C, gas mark 4) for 50 to 60 minutes. The middle can be slightly damp when it comes out of the oven, but you want to watch for the full-pie jiggle. If you can create a cross-pie wave by jiggling it, it isn't done. A localized center jiggle is fine, though. The pie will carry over and finish cooking that last little jiggle.

Let the pie sit for at least an hour.

Yield: 1 pie (8 servings)

Anne Fidanza's Easter Ricotta Pie

This is a traditional Italian pie that graces tables on holidays. It uses a variation on a shortbread crust that is sweet with eggs, so there is no need to blind-bake the crust.

One extra step: Drain the ricotta so your crust doesn't become soggy. Line a colander with cheesecloth, put it over a bowl or sink, and pour the cheese in it to drain for at least an hour. Do not press it; just let gravity do its thing. This step helps create a firm pie.

This pie uses a variation on a shortbread crust. It is more cohesive than traditional pie crust, since the butter you use is softened, and the eggs are a wonderful bind for the crust. This crust is more stable and consistent; it is not about flakiness.

Preheat the oven to 350°F (180°C, gas mark 4).

Bottom Crust

Pull out one of your chilled crusts from the refrigerator. Roll like a regular pie crust, moving it a quarter turn to create a circle. Roll the crust out to about 13 inches (33 cm), flip it in half, and put it in the pie plate. Lift the edges so the crust is flush with the pie plate. Trim the edges to ¼ inch (6 mm) and flute. Chill.

Filling

Put your drained ricotta cheese in a medium-size bowl and begin to break it up so it become less chunky. Add the sugar and salt and keep mixing. Incorporate the eggs one at a time; it's important to make sure one egg is mixed in before adding another one. Finish with the lemon and orange zest and booze. Set aside while you roll out the top crust.

Crust (Follow the instructions on page 32.)

- ½ cup (112 g) unsalted butter, softened
- ¼ cup (50 g) granulated sugar
- 2 eggs
- 1 teaspoon (5 ml) vanilla extract
- 2½ cups (310 g) all-purpose flour
- 1 teaspoon baking powder
- ¼ teaspoon (2 g) kosher salt

Filling

- 2 pounds (910 g) ricotta, room temperature, drained for an hour
- 1½ cups (300 g) granulated sugar
- ½ teaspoon (3 g) kosher salt
- 8 whole eggs, room temperature
  zest of 1 lemon and 1 orange
  shot of Grand Marnier, brandy, or your favorite elixir

- -

This recipe comes from chef Caroline Fidanza, one of the owners of Saltie in Williamsburg, Brooklyn. She is the reason for the boom of whole animal programs in restaurants and the borough of Brooklyn's investment in local farmers. I should be thanking her. Instead I've stolen her mother's Easter pie recipe.

- -

Top Crust

Get the other chilled crust and roll out as you would for a lattice. Pour the filling into the pie plate and construct the lattice as instructed on pages 50–52.

Put in the preheated oven. After 30 minutes, rotate the pie 180 degrees. Check in another 20 minutes. Just the center of the pie should jiggle. Cook for 5 to 10 more minutes depending on the jiggle.

Pull the pie and let sit for at least an hour.

Yield: 1 pie (8 servings)

Bourbon Pecan Pie

Crust

Single Pie Crust (page 19), chilled

Filling

½ cup (112 g) unsalted melted butter

1 ½ cups (165 g) coarsely chopped pecans, the fresher the better, toasted

3 extra-large eggs, room temperature

½ cup (60 g) packed light brown sugar

½ cup (100 g) granulated sugar

½ cup (170 g) light corn syrup

½ cup (170 g) dark corn syrup

¼ cup (85 g) molasses (blackstrap)

¼ cup (60 ml) bourbon—but not more!!

1 teaspoon (5 ml) vanilla

½ teaspoon (3 g) kosher salt

Prebake tools

aluminum foil

baking beans

Many variations of nuts, sugar, and eggs can inhabit a pie crust and be tantalizing. To one person it may seem of little consequence—just pick a pie and run with it—but to someone else, it's the minutiae that illuminate our taste memories. This is the food at its best, when it transports us. This all seems like bunk, until you see it happen, or have it happen to you.

Tamara Reynolds runs a supper club in Astoria, Queens. She has written a book about the lost art of throwing a dinner party, and is regularly sought for her opinion on food, wine, and service. In other words, she's got it covered. Luckily she is a dear friend. This is her recipe, and here are her thoughts:

"I make this pie every Thanksgiving for my friend Grant, who was raised on a farm in Arkansas. He swears to God that it is the ghost of his late mother's pecan pie; I don't know about that, but I do know that I have never seen such joy over a piece of pie. It is always a pleasure to make it for him."

Preheat the oven to 425°F (220°C, gas mark 7).

Bottom Crust

Roll out your chilled pie crust to ⅛-inch (3 mm) thick. It should be about 13 inches (33 cm) in diameter. Place in your pie pan per the instructions in chapter 3. Trim the edges so there is no more than ¼ inch (6 mm) of overhang. Lift and crimp the overhang along the rim of the pie pan. Prick the bottom and the sides of the crust with a regular fork to prevent bubbles. Try to not pierce through the crust. If you can, chill your crust in the freezer for at least 15 minutes. If not, chill it in the refrigerator for at least 20 minutes. It is important for the crust to be very cold and the fat to re-form and firm up.

Pull your pie plate out of the refrigerator and place your foil in it. It should sit flush with the plate, come up along the rim, and fold down to cover the edges. This foil protects the crust from overbrowning, but you do not want the foil pressed securely to the edges. Place your baking beans in the bottom and level them out. Put the crust in the oven.

Bake the crust for 15 minutes at 425°F (220°C, gas mark 7). Then pull out the crust, lower your oven to 350°F (180°C, gas mark 4), and carefully lift the aluminum foil by the edges off your crust with the beans in it. Put your crust back in the oven for 10 minutes. Pull and let cool a bit.

Preheat the oven to 375°F (190°C, gas mark 5).

Filling

Melt your butter and let cool. Arrange your nuts on the bottom of the par-baked crust. Whisk together the eggs until homogenized and add the white and brown sugars, then the corn syrups, molasses, bourbon, vanilla, melted butter, and salt. Pour the mixture over the nuts and carefully transfer to the oven. The pecans will float.

Bake for 35 to 40 minutes or until the pie is set. A little wiggle in the middle is all right; the pie will continue cooking at it sits. Let cool at least 1 hour.

Yield: 1 pie (8 servings)

Lemon Honeysuckle Pie

Crust

Graham cracker crumb crust
(page 29), chilled

Filling

¼ cup (85 g) honeycomb with honey

¼ cup (60 g) packed light brown sugar

2 tablespoons (40 g) maple syrup

1 package (8 ounces [228 g]) full-fat
cream cheese, softened

zest and juice of 2 lemons

½ teaspoon (6 g) kosher salt

½ cup (120 ml) cold heavy cream

¼ cup (50 g) granulated sugar

3 egg whites, room temperature

This icebox pie is great for those summer days you can barely consider turning the oven on. You just need it on long enough to bake your cracker crust. The rest of the work goes to the mixer and the freezer. It's always a triumph when you can transform everyday ingredients to something airy. If you can find raw honeycomb, it is a real treat. It is completely edible, and it also adds some nice bits to chew in this pie.

Preheat the oven to 375°F (190°C, gas mark 5).

Bottom Crust

Make a graham cracker crumb crust as instructed on page 29. Chill it for 10 minutes and then bake off. Let cool for an hour.

Filling

Cut up the honeycomb. Take the side of your knife, put it on top of the honeycomb, and smear it back and forth to break it down. Put the whole mess with the honey, brown sugar, and maple syrup in your mixer, or use your hand mixer to make a paste out of them. Add the room-temperature cream cheese and let them all mix together on medium speed for a few minutes. Add the lemon zest, lemon juice, and salt. Mix well.

Whip the cold heavy cream in a cold, dry bowl. Heavy cream will not whip in a damp bowl. After the cream doubles in volume slowly add the ¼ cup (50 g) granulated sugar until you have stiff peaks. Mix with the lemon cream cheese mixture. Refrigerate.

Clean and dry your bowl and beaters well. Egg whites are very sensitive to residue and moisture. Beat the egg whites until they become foamy. Begin at a lower speed until their proteins begin to unravel and bubble up and the volume increases. Up the speed to medium, and whip up to just stiff peaks. Test the peaks by dipping your index finger in them. If they keep, they're good.

Add the chilled filling in 3 batches along the edge of the bowl. Use a rubber spatula to fold the egg whites and the filling together. Do not overmix. Just gently move your spatula along the perimeter of the bowl down and up and once every while across the middle.

Chill

Pour the filling into the room-temperature crust and put in the refrigerator for an hour so the filling firms up. It is best to slice cold pies with a hot, clean knife. Put your knife in a glass of hot water before and after every slice. Always wipe clean.

Yield: 1 pie (8 servings)

Corn Buttermilk Pie

Crust

Single Pie Crust (page 19), chilled

Filling

1 stick (½ cup [112 g]) unsalted butter, melted

2 large or 3 small ears of sweet corn, shaved

3 eggs, room temperature

1 cup (235 ml) buttermilk, room temperature

1 cup (200 g) granulated sugar

1 teaspoon kosher salt

zest and juice of 1 lemon

Wash

1 egg white

Prebake tools

aluminum foil

baking beans

- - - - - - - - - - - - - - - - - - - -

This pie tastes like sweet, colored cereal O's. There is something in my DNA capable of replicating the most processed food without intention. I could mix seven different cheeses and still make a macaroni and cheese that's a dead ringer for the boxed version. I've pickled almost-ripened green tomatoes before, and they were reminiscent of canned spaghetti. I made watermelon rind pickles that were homemade versions of watermelon candy. In the business we call this a happy accident.

- - - - - - - - - - - - - - - - - - - -

Pairing corn with custard makes sense; the sweetness of the corn reads as a dessert, and used with buttermilk, it feels like country flavors in a classy place.

Sweet corn can balance out the tanginess of the buttermilk. Or rather that pitch of the buttermilk can add another level of flavor to the sweetness in a gentle manner.

Preheat the oven to 425°F (220°C, gas mark 7).

Bottom Crust

Roll out your chilled pie crust to ⅛-inch (3 mm) thick and about 13 inches (33 cm) in diameter. Place in your pie pan as shown in chapter 3. Trim the edges so there is no more than ¼ inch (6 mm) of overhang. Lift and crimp the overhang along the rim. Prick the bottom and the sides of the crust to prevent bubbles. Try not to pierce through the crust. Chill your crust in the freezer for at least 15 minutes or in the refrigerator for at least 20 minutes. It is important for the crust to be very cold and the fat to re-form and firm up.

Pull your pie plate out of the refrigerator and place your foil in it. It should sit flush with the plate, come up along the rim, and fold down to cover the edges. This foil protects the crust from overbrowning, but do not press the foil to the edges. Place your baking beans in the bottom and bake the crust for 15 minutes at 425°F (220°C, gas mark 7). Then pull out the crust, lower your oven to 350°F (180°C, gas mark 4), and carefully lift the aluminum foil by the edges off your crust with the beans in it. Put your crust back in the oven for 10 minutes. Pull and let cool a bit. Brush the crust with the egg white wash.

Filling

Melt your butter. Shuck the corn and pick the silk out of the kernels. Place a clean kitchen towel on your surface, hold the ear of corn by the handle God gave it, and put the butt of the corn on the kitchen towel. The ear of corn is perpendicular to the table. (a) Hold it firmly with your nondominant hand, and with your sharpest knife in your good hand, shave the kernels off the cob (b, c, d, e). The kitchen towel should trap them. Take the back of a regular butter knife and scrape it back and forth across the cob (f). This is called milking the cob; it gets all the magical corn flavor out of the cob.

Mix the room-temperature eggs and buttermilk. Whisk in the sugar, salt, lemon zest, and juice and add the butter in a stream. Finish with the corn and pour into the cooled pie shell. Remember, cold eggs and a hot pie are not friends.

Bake in the 350°F (180°C, gas mark 4) oven for an hour. Check at 30 minutes and give it a turn. The pie is done when just the center jiggles.

Pull and let set for an hour before serving.

Chocolate Olive Oil Pie

Crust

Single Pie Crust (page 19), chilled

Filling

5 ounces dark chocolate (I like 72 percent)

2 whole eggs, room temperature

2 yolks, room temperature

¾ cup (175 ml) extra-virgin olive oil

¼ cup (60 ml) buttermilk, room temperature

1¼ cups (250 g) granulated sugar

1 teaspoon (6 g) kosher salt

3 tablespoons (27 g) cornmeal

Wash

1 egg white

Prebake tools

aluminum foil

baking beans

- - - - - - - - - - - - - - - - - - -

I sprinkle sea salt on top of this pie, which adds a tasty, addictive element to the pie. If you are hesitant to add salt to your chocolate, try it once and decide—a good approach toward many things in this world.

- - - - - - - - - - - - - - - - - - -

This pie is a mixture of a chess pie and an olive oil cake. It's a dense, rich filling with an unexpected crunchy top crust. In the tradition of a chocolate chess pie I use cornmeal, but use olive oil as the main fat in the filling.

If executed correctly, the top crusts over and the filling swells as it bakes and then falls when the pie comes out of the oven. Take a natural top crust anytime you don't have to make it.

This pie is the first pie I really understood the importance of time and temperature. Whenever I tried to rush the pie, by not allowing the par-baked crust to cool a bit, or getting the eggs to room temperature, or letting the chocolate cool a bit, I didn't achieve that wonderful top crust. And while it all tastes great together, it is that top crust that really separates this pie from being great to being some sort of brownie pie.

1 In a medium-size bowl get your eggs and yolks together. Whisk well, then slowly add the olive oil in a steady stream so it is emulsified with the eggs. Add the buttermilk, sugar, salt, and cornmeal. Mix well.

Preheat the oven to 425°F (220°C, gas mark 7).

Bottom Crust

Roll out your chilled pie crust to ⅛-inch (3 mm) thick and about 15 inches (38 cm) in diameter. Place in your pie pan per the instructions in chapter 3. Trim the edges so there is no more than ¼ inch (6 mm) of overhang. Lift and crimp the overhang along the rim. Chill your crust in the freezer for at least 15 minutes or in the refrigerator for at least 20 minutes. It is important for the crust to be very cold and the fat to re-form and firm up.

Pull your pie plate out of the refrigerator and place your foil in it. It should sit flush with the plate, come up along the rim, and fold down to cover the edges. This foil protects the crust from overbrowning, but do not press the foil to the edges. Place your baking beans in the bottom and level them out. Put the crust in the oven.

Bake the crust for 15 minutes at 425°F (220°C, gas mark 7). Then pull out the crust, lower your oven to 350°F (180°C, gas mark 4), and carefully lift the aluminum foil by the edges off your crust with the beans

2 Once the chocolate is melted, allow it to cool and then add it to the dairy mixture and whisk together well. Bang the bowl down hard on the countertop to release any air bubbles.

in it. Put your crust back in the oven for 10 minutes. Pull out and let cool a bit. After 10 minutes, lightly brush the crust with the beaten egg white to patch any holes.

Filling

Put a few inches of water in a sauce pot and heat up over a high flame then turn down to a simmer. Weigh the chocolate and put it in a bowl that sets atop the sauce pot to melt. The bottom of the bowl should not touch the water. Mix the chocolate a bit as it melts.

Pour the filling into a cooled partially baked crust and put in a 325°F (170°C, gas mark 3) oven. After 30 minutes, turn the pie 180 degrees. The pie is done when the filling is set. The filling of the pie will be risen above the edges of the crust with a light brown top crust. It will fall as it cools. Sprinkle 2 tablespoons (36 g) sea salt on top. Let rest an hour.

Yield: 1 pie (8 servings)

Chocolate Caramel Pecan Pie

Caramel

Yields 2 cups (680 g)

2 cups (400 g) sugar

½ cup (120 ml) water

⅔ cup (160 ml) heavy cream, room temperature

2 sticks (1 cup) (224 g) unsalted butter, room temperature

1 teaspoon (6 g) salt

2 teaspoons vanilla extract

Crust

Shortbread Crust (page 32), baked

Filling

1½ cups (165 g) unbroken pecan halves

2 cups (680 g) caramel, room temperature

3 eggs, room temperature

1 teaspoon (5 ml) vanilla extract

1 tablespoon (15 ml) bourbon

5 ounces (140 g) high-quality semisweet chocolate, finely chopped, 50 to 60 percent cocoa content; much more than that has a bitter burn in the pie

Caramel is a great tool to have in your dessert arsenal, yet another impressive mutation of things most likely in your kitchen right now. An important part of making caramel is being careful. Hot sugar burns, sticks, and hurts. When you add the cream and butter to the hot sugar, add it in a way that will not splash up on your hands or arms. Be thoughtful. You can make this caramel days in advance, too.

- -

Eben Burr is an astonishingly talented baker who has a birthday party every year where he takes time off from work, bakes for three days straight, and then hosts an evening for his friends with the lot. He is also known for ordering pie as an appetizer. He really knows how to write a recipe too.

- -

Make the caramel in advance. It takes too long to cool if you make it at the same time as the rest. It lasts forever if tightly sealed and refrigerated.

Put the sugar and water in a small saucepan over medium heat and cook for 15 to 30 minutes depending on your range until it starts to turn an amber color. (Sometimes it takes forever; don't sweat it. The worst that can happen is it dries up and you have to add a teaspoon of water.) It may start to crystallize on top or edges as it gets close to caramelizing. If this happens, increase the temperature slightly or put a lid on it, but watch carefully, as it will start to caramelize quickly.

Do not move the pan until the browning just begins, then swirl as it starts becoming a golden amber color. (You may want to compensate by bringing up the flame, since you are moving it further from the heat source while swirling.)

Remove from heat when it is an amber, not brown, color and IMMEDIATELY whisk in the cream and butter. It may clump, but continue whisking and it will melt. Add the salt and vanilla.

Preheat the oven to 375°F (190°C, gas mark 5).

Filling

Place the pecans in a bowl, drizzle 2 tablespoons (40 g) of caramel over them, and gently toss to get a thin coating. Space them out on a piece of parchment paper on a sheet pan. Place them in the oven for 10 to 15 minutes, depending on your oven. Allow to cool to room temperature on parchment paper, but off of the hot sheet pan while you prepare the rest of the guts.

Place the sheet pan back in the oven to stay hot.

Beat the 3 eggs. Add the remaining caramel, vanilla, and bourbon and whisk until fully combined.

Cover the bottom of the pie crust evenly with the chocolate. Cover with the caramel-egg mixture.

Starting at the center of the pie, place the pecans facing outward in a cross, making an X in the middle of the pie. They will stay afloat if you place them gently. From the center continue to fan out the pecans (all in the same direction), creating a radiating pattern from the center out, keeping them as close together as possible. Once you have reached the edge with the pecans, you have to cut a few to make sure the whole surface is covered.

Place the pie on hot cookie sheet in the oven and bake until the center is just firm. It will bulge, but return to shape when cooled.

Yield: 1 pie (8 servings)

Shaker Lemon Pie

Crust

Single Pie Crust (page 19), chilled

Filling

3 lemons sliced as thinly as possible
while still keeping shape

2 cups (400 g) granulated sugar

4 whole eggs, room temperature

¾ cup (170 g) packed brown sugar

1 teaspoon kosher salt

Wash

1 egg white

Prebake tools

aluminum foil

baking beans

The food, furniture, and gentle fanaticism of the Shakers hold a place in my heart. Originating in England as Quakers, they were named as such for the manner in which they prayed: They shook. Led by a woman called Ann Lee, they split from the Quakers and England, moved to the United States, and set themselves up in farming communities based on gender equality.

They invented many great things: the broom as we know it, the clothespin, the circular saw, and a giant rotating oven with a capacity for sixty pies. Like many agrarian societies they ate with gusto, their version of work hard, play hard, and really utilized what the season offered.

I've had my eye on this pie for a while, intrigued by a pie so ballsy to use sliced lemons but wondering how it would really taste. I've always found the recipe's instructions a bit paltry. I've tested it, and this version should give you a tangy pie somewhere between a custard and a curd. The lemon slices become soft and edible, and the ones on top end up with a candied quality. And it's pretty. Real pretty.

It's important to prebake the crust. Eggs are an important part of this recipe because they create the creaminess, but in my experience with eggs they do not participate well with temperatures over 375°F (190°C, gas mark 5). This is a tangy pie; you can't keep lemon down forever, and a little goes a long way. You need thinly sliced lemons, so they're almost transparent.

A mandolin is a piece of equipment that revolutionizes this pie. You can get really beautiful, evenly cut slices, which is quite important because they can be more edible. If you come across Meyer lemons, they are perfect for this pie. If you don't, well, we will make do with regular lemons.

Take the time to lay out the lemon slices in a circular pattern—it creates the pie's structure.

Preparation of Lemons

The night before you bake this pie, slice the lemons as thinly as possible while they still keep their shape. A mandolin (Japanese slicing tool) is a perfect tool for this. It should be sharp enough so the pulp holds in the rind, but you should also be able to see through the slices. If there are seeds, gently push them out of the slices with a knife. It only *seems* overwhelming to deseed these lemon slices; once you focus, it takes all of 5 minutes. Put the slices in a small bowl and mix gently (so they retain their hard-fought-for shape!) with the 2 cups (400 g) of granulated sugar. Refrigerate overnight.

Note: The longer the lemons sit in the sugar the more edible they become. You can do this the morning of baking the pie, but they should be out at room temperature with the sugar to move things along. Allow at least 5 hours sitting time in the kitchen.

Preheat the oven to 425°F (220°C, gas mark 7).

Bottom Crust

Roll out your chilled pie crust to ⅛-inch (3 mm) thick. It should be about 15 inches (38 cm) in diameter. Place in your pie pan per the instructions in chapter 3. Trim the edges so there is no more than ¼ inch (6 mm) of overhang. Lift and crimp the overhang along the rim of the pie pan. Chill pie crust ideally in your freezer for at least 20 minutes, or 30 minutes in your refrigerator. It is really important for your crust to set again and the fat to refirm before you prebake.

Pull your pie plate out of the refrigerator and place your foil in it. It should sit flush with the plate, come up along the rim, and fold down to cover the edges. This foil protects the crust from overbrowning, but you do not want the foil pressed securely to the edges. Place your baking beans in the bottom and level them out. Put the crust in the oven. While you're at it, pull your lemons in sugar too. Bake the crust for 20 minutes at 425°F (220°C, gas mark 7). Then pull out the crust, lower your oven to 375°F (190°C, gas mark 5), and carefully lift the aluminum foil by the edges off your crust with the beans in it. Put your crust back in the oven for 15 minutes. Check at 7 minutes and turn it 180 degrees.

Whisk the 4 whole eggs at room temperature in a bowl until completely homogenized, when the egg yolks and whites are mixed. Add the brown sugar and salt and mix well.

Check your crust. The edges may be a little darker than the rest, but it should be set and very light in color. The bottom is more likely bubbly a little bit and looks shiny. Let it cook a bit more, 5 minutes at the most if the bottom is more shiny than matte. Then take the crust out and let it rest for 10 minutes. Lower the oven to 350°F (180°C, gas mark 4).

Whip your egg white and wash it on the bottom and sides of the crust. It functions as insurance against gaps. Layer your lemon slices flush with the sides and circling in. Add whatever is left in the bowl to your bowl of eggs, sugar, and salt. Quickly whisk together and pour over the lemon slices.

Note: When you prebake crusts and use eggs, it is very important for the crust to cool a bit and for your mixture to be room temperature. If you put a cold mixture into a hot crust you are cooking some spots without intention.

Place the pie in the oven. After 30 minutes, rotate 180 degrees. The pie is done after an hour. Give it a shake; it should move solidly throughout with just a loose jiggle in the middle. This little jiggle will set up with carryover cooking.

Let set 1 hour. Serve with whipped cream or vanilla ice cream, just a little something to offset the lemon.

Yield: 1 pie (8 servings)

- -

When you pick lemons for this pie, get a few extra as back-ups. It is really important that the lemon is not brown inside. Don't choose the largest lemons either; they tend to have thicker pith than the smaller ones.

- -

Chess Pie

Crust

Single Pie Crust (page 19), chilled

Filling

3 large eggs, separated,
room temperature

¾ cup (150 g) granulated sugar

⅓ cup (75 g) unsalted butter, melted

⅛ teaspoon (6 g) kosher salt

¼ cup (31 g) unbleached all-purpose flour

½ cup (120 ml) buttermilk,
room temperature

1 teaspoon (5 ml) cider vinegar

1 teaspoon (2 g) finely grated orange zest

Prebake

aluminum foil

baking beans

These two chess pie recipes come from Michelle Warner, who is some sort of culinary superhero. I never realized all the skills she has under her belt, especially in a world that has its fair share of puffy chested superstars. She is a recipe tester, food stylist, and patient coordinator for the frazzled mind. She is also an excellent cook and recipe maker.

When you fold egg whites into a custard, think of the actual gentle motion of folding a sheet, of trying to maintain the air you've just whisked into the egg whites. You don't want to diminish them with a harsh, cutting motion. You want to fold these two entities together in a kind, circular motion so you can maintain the volume. Pour the mixture into the partially baked pie shell.

Chess pie is the ultimate staple pie. If you peered into your kitchen right now, you probably have most of these ingredients, which is why this pie is a real gem.

There are a few legends about where the name comes from, but I think the one that rings most true (and the one I like the most) is that once, the unnamed baker of a chess pie, when asked what is what, just shrugged her shoulders and said, "It's just pie." It's chess pie.

Preheat the oven to 425°F (220°C, gas mark 7).

Bottom Crust

Roll out your chilled pie crust to ⅛-inch (3 mm) thick and about 13 inches (33 cm) in diameter. Place in your pie pan per the instructions in chapter 3. Trim the edges so there is no more than ¼ inch (6 mm) of overhang. Lift and crimp the overhang along the rim. Prick the bottom and the sides of the crust to prevent bubbles. Try to not pierce through the crust. If you can, chill your crust in the freezer for at least 15 minutes or chill it in the refrigerator for at least 20 minutes. It is important for the crust to be very cold and the fat to re-form and firm up.

Make sure your oven rack is in the middle or lower half of your oven.

Pull your pie plate out of the refrigerator and place your foil in it. It should sit flush with the plate, come up along the rim, and fold down to cover the edges. This foil protects the crust from overbrowning, but do not press the foil to the edges. Place your baking beans in the bottom and level them out.

Bake the crust for 15 minutes at 425°F (220°C, gas mark 7). Pull out the crust, lower your oven to 350°F (180°C, gas mark 4), and carefully lift the aluminum foil by the edges off your crust with the beans in it. Put your crust back in the oven for 10 minutes. Pull and let cool a bit.

Increase the oven temperature to 375°F (190°C, gas mark 5).

Filling

Separate your eggs carefully. Put the whites in a clean, dry bowl.

In a bowl, whisk together the sugar, melted butter, and salt. Add the egg yolks one at a time, beating until smooth after each addition. Stir in the flour, buttermilk, vinegar, and orange zest, mixing well.

With a clean, dry whisk beat your egg whites to medium stiff peaks. It is important that the bowl and whisk are dry, and it is really helpful for beating egg whites if they are room temperature. Fold the stiff whites into the custard, ideally using a rubber spatula.

Bake the pie until the top is golden brown and domed and the filling is firm, 20 to 30 minutes. Transfer to a wire rack and let cool completely.

Serve at room temperature.

Yield : 1 pie (8 servings)

Cranberry Chess Pie

Crust

Single Pie Crust (page 19), chilled

Filling

3 large eggs, separated,
  room temperature

1 cup (200 g) granulated sugar

⅓ cup (75 g) unsalted butter, melted

⅛ teaspoon kosher salt

¼ cup (31 g) unbleached all-purpose flour

½ cup (120 ml) buttermilk,
  room temperature

1 teaspoon (5 ml) cider vinegar

1 teaspoon (2 g) finely grated orange zest

2 cups (220 g) fresh or frozen cranberries,
  coarsely chopped, leaving ¼ cup
  (25 g) whole

Prebake

aluminum foil

baking beans

Cranberries can be difficult to bake with because they are really quite tart, but mixed with the chess pie they provide a great foil to the sweetness. This version of the chess pie uses a touch more sugar to counter the cranberries' tanginess. Other fruit with that same bite would work well in this chess pie, like sour cherries.

Preheat the oven to 425°F (220°C, gas mark 7).

Bottom Crust

Roll out your chilled pie crust to ⅛-inch (3 mm) thick. It should be about 13 inches (33 cm) in diameter. Place in your pie pan per the instructions in chapter 3. Trim the edges so there is no more than ¼ inch (6 mm) of overhang. Lift and crimp the overhang along the rim of the pie pan. Prick the bottom and the sides of the crust with a regular fork to prevent bubbles. Try to not pierce through the crust. If you can, chill your crust in the freezer for at least 15 minutes. If not, chill it in the refrigerator for at least 20 minutes. It is important for the crust to be very cold and the fat to re-form and firm up.

Make sure your oven rack is in the middle or lower half of your oven.

Pull your pie plate out of the refrigerator and place your foil in it. It should sit flush with the plate, come up along the rim, and fold down to cover the edges. This foil protects the crust from overbrowning, but you do not want the foil pressed securely to the edges. Place your baking beans in the bottom and level them out. Put the crust in the oven.

Bake the crust for 15 minutes at 425°F (220°C, gas mark 7). Then pull out the crust, lower your oven to 350°F (180°C, gas mark 4), and carefully lift the aluminum foil by the edges off your crust with the beans in it. Put your crust back in the oven for 10 minutes. Pull and let cool a bit.

Increase oven temperature to 375°F (190°C, gas mark 5).

Filling

Separate your eggs carefully. Put the whites in a clean, dry bowl.

In a bowl, whisk together the sugar, melted butter, and salt. Add the egg yolks one at a time, beating until smooth after each addition. Stir in the flour, buttermilk, vinegar, and orange zest, mixing well.

With a clean, dry whisk beat your egg whites to medium stiff peaks. It is important that the bowl and whisk are dry, and it is really helpful for beating egg whites if they are room temperature. Fold the stiff whites into the custard, ideally using a rubber spatula. When you fold egg whites into a custard, think of the actual gentle motion of folding a sheet, of trying to maintain the air you've just whisked into the egg whites. You don't want to diminish them with harsh cutting motions; you want to fold these two entities together in a kind, circular motion so you can maintain the volume.

Stir in the cranberries and scrape the mixture into the partially baked pie shell.

Bake the pie until the top is golden brown and domed and the filling is firm, 25 to 35 minutes. Transfer to a wire rack and let cool completely.

Serve at room temperature.

Yield: 1 pie (8 servings)

CHAPTER 6

Savory Pies,
Meat Pies,
Pot Pies, Oh, My!

There are sweet pies and there are savory pies. The essence of savory pies is necessity and nourishment. That is the spirit in which I approach them.

Savory pies are more omnipresent; every culture has its version on a large and on a small scale. You can tell where a culture lives by what they are putting in a crust. Small pies, called hand pies, pasties, or empanadas are great foods on the go.

Pot pies strike a chord in a person's heart. Their rich, rustic nature evokes some childhood memory, or a night in front of a fireplace, or an evening with a TV tray and an empty box of frozen pot pie. A pot pie is the pinnacle of comfort foods, so cozy it's practically a sweater. Pot pies can take on a multitude of flavors and well utilize the timeliest of vegetables. The classic savory pies take advantage of the chillier months' bounty, namely root vegetables.

Savory pies require more preparation and cooking than sweet pies. They show the shine of a cook, an ability to take leftovers or what is around and stretch it. They often require braising the meat, since these cuts of meat cannot braise in the crust. They are labors of love—the love of great-tasting food. As the saying goes, you either have time or money, if you're lucky, so the least expensive meats take the most amount of time to cook. These endeavors require reliable pots, knife skills, ingenuity, and some planning.

They also really like to be made in cast-iron pans. The beauty of the pot pie is, in general: Once the crust is cooked, the pie is done. They follow the same general rule as sweet pies—if it tastes good in the bowl it will taste good baked in the crust. Savory pies, however, encompass a different approach than dessert pies, so let's go through them.

Savory Ingredients

Savory pies take everything humble, tough cuts and root vegetables, marry them in a crust, and nourish us.

Vegetables

It's possible to use any combination of vegetables in pot pies; don't limit yourself to just potatoes. In fact, you can make just a vegetable pie. In most cases the vegetables need to be cooked before they go into the crust.

The cooking methods used for savory pies have little to do with pastry or baking. They have everything to do with roasting meat and making soup and cutting vegetables—making dinner type of stuff. This kind of cooking needs your brain to begin considering how food acts and what it needs. You cannot just put a bunch of raw food in a pie crust and expect it to cook through in an hour. Essentially when you are a baking a pot pie, you are just baking the crust. Most of the food inside of it does not cook through.

Cooking Vegetables for Savory Pies

A poorly cooked, or undercooked, vegetable can influence your eating experience just as much as an under- or tragically overcooked piece of meat. Vegetables, when done well, can blow your mind. For pies, most of them need to be cooked before entering the crust.

Consider the vegetable and think about whether the vegetables you are using need to be cooked prior to the baking of the pie. If so, how do they want to be cooked? If you are using a classic French *mirepoix*—onions, carrots, and celery—then you should cook them before baking. They influence the flavor of your food positively when they are sautéed together, becoming soft and aromatic.

Root vegetables are nearly synonymous with savory pies. These include the aforementioned onions and carrots, but also turnips, potatoes, celeriac, yams, and rutabaga. Many of these vegetables are grown throughout the year, barring freezing, but are often available in the colder months. Food that grows in dirt is pretty sturdy fare.

You must cook root vegetables before they go in the pie. When you prepare these vegetables, it is important to cut everything the same size so they cook at the same rate. The best ways to cook root vegetables is to sauté them in butter, olive oil, or another delicious fat on your stovetop, or to roast them in your oven lightly covered with olive oil. Sautéing works well if the vegetables are cut or are naturally an inch (2.5 cm) in length or less. Bigger than that and I think roasting them in an oven is great. They cook better in the oven.

Small potatoes can be roasted whole. Roasting brings out a delicious flavor and lends a satisfying crust to the skin.

Do not boil your vegetables in water. That does nothing for flavor; in fact, the water leaches flavor from the vegetables.

Leeks also require cooking. The most usable and edible part of the leek, the white and light green section, is sometimes maddeningly small. Leeks demonstrate the importance of utilizing the most from our food; they can be expensive with little. Keep the tops of leeks, the dark green parts, to use for your stocks as your onion element. This stretches them. Leeks like to be sautéed and also braised in wine and stock until they are tender.

Peppers, both hot and mild, like to be sautéed before going in the pie. Their texture and flavor improve with this extra step.

Mushrooms are vastly improved when they're cooked—sautéed or roasted—before baking in a pie. Mushrooms cannot achieve that wonderful umami richness that allows them to so intently enrich anything they're added to without being cooked ahead of the crust. They may seem delicate enough to just cook in the crust, but they will not achieve that depth of flavor.

What Goes in Raw

The vegetables best left alone are the delicate ones, such as corn, green and red tomatoes, zucchini, and peas. Their time in the crust is enough to cook them for the pie and still be complementary. These are the vegetables I like cooked the least, where just a touch of heat and steam will do the trick. Corn with a little tooth to it is delicious, while a crunchy potato is still just raw. Regarding tomatoes, cook them if they are to function as a sauce, but if you want to them to retain some of their raw pop, just toss them in the crust with the rest of the filling. This also applies to green tomatoes, which I love for the tartness.

Meat

Meat also needs to be cooked for the filling of the pot pie. Let's not chance that one. And not every meat, love it as you may, is appropriate for savory pies. Much as there is an appropriate soundtrack for every moment of our lives, even the sound of silence, there is an appropriate meat for every pie, even none. Perhaps that meat is already cooked, be it last night's roast or chicken. Meat in pies is an element; it does not have to be the most dominant part. The more luxury cuts of a cow or pig are being wasted if they are used for pies. It's a gesture that comes across as showy, rather than delicious.

PIG'S FEET AND *MIREPOIX*

Meat pies use ground beef, but really you could use any ground meat you like or a combination of them. The important part of meat pies is to use ground meat with a significant percentage of fat; the same kind of grind you use for hamburgers or meatballs is ideal. You don't want a really lean grind—your pie will be too dry.

Braising meats are excellent for pies; they are affordable, flavorful cuts of meat that have a lot of the connective tissue collagen. Every cut of meat has an exemplary manner in which to be utilized; to wit, filet mignon, sirloin, and chops, in general need not be used for pot pies. To braise meat is to first sear it off and then let it cook at a low temperature with any combination of stock, beer and wine, and water if need be. You may also add various aromatics to inform the flavor. You can add *mirepoix*, sautéed onions, carrots, and celery for their aromatic natures.

After a period of time, which is dependent on the size of the cut but is usually no less than an hour, the meat becomes tender. It's not that everything melts away; it's that everything melts together, and the longer the meat can sit in the braising liquid and cook, (hence the low temperature), the more delicious it becomes. Braising meat is more forgiving that searing and cooking the more expensive cuts, and the end result can be astonishing. Generally the less money you spend on meat the more time you have to cook it, but here if you have the right pot and set the temperature correctly, it is low maintenance.

Cuts that are great for braising are parts of the animals that do a lot of work: the neck, shoulder, leg, hocks, and tail. It's nice to know that work pays off. The beauty of braising meat is the output is twofold: not only is the meat cooking, but it is making its own sauce. And pies need sauce. Actually, pies need gravy, something thicker than sauce to coat the food and be one with it. It's a fine line between gummy and runny, and braising liquid is that line. All of the tough parts of the meat melt down to give body to the braising liquid, so it ends up as a combination of whatever liquids you put with the meat in the beginning, whatever the vegetables gave, and all the collagen and fat.

Dutch Ovens

It's important to have the right pot. This pot is called a Dutch oven and comes in a variety of sizes. Depending on how you feel about size, you should get one that holds anywhere from 4 quarts to 8 quarts. They are one of the most versatile things to have in your kitchen, and their durability is unheralded. I have one from the late 1800s. There are many fabulous things about Dutch ovens: They are made of cast iron (some are enameled), and this is really important because cast iron holds heat really well, disperses it as evenly as possible, and has a thick bottom. This bottom is important for achieving high heats for browning with your pan and not burn or scorch the pan or the food. Also, once you get the hang of it and find the sweet spot, you can just let your braise simmer along at a low rate unattended. There are many pans out there to buy and few you actually need. This is one of them.

The meat you braise for pot pie is so intense and rich that you don't need a lot of it in the pie, especially as it's accompanied by its braising liquid.

Beyond braising cuts pies can use ground meat, ideally beef or pork, or a combination of the two. The cooking time is negligible compared to shoulders and necks, and the meat tastes great when you allow it to have a good fat content, at least 25 percent. Fat is flavor; do not forget that.

Cooking Chicken and Poultry

You can't talk about pies without talking about chicken pot pie. Chicken is less forgiving to cook than, say, a pork shoulder. (A pork shoulder tends to be consistent in its qualities.) Poultry is difficult because often we are cooking the entire animal, and different parts of an animal beget different cooking doneness. The dark meat of poultry is the part with fat, and cooked through at a higher temperature than the white meat. It is about a ten-degree difference in doneness, except the dark meat has the grace period of having fat, while the white meat has a smaller window of temperature to become overdone, dry. And medium-rare chicken is not an accepted dinner in this world. This is a very common poultry concern.

So the question becomes which is the most suitable way to cook a chicken for chicken pot pie? Just as every task has the proper vessel, every food has the proper preparation, and in this case, it is chicken in a pot. There are more ways to cook a chicken than fingers on a hand. For this discussion, let's keep the chicken in the pot the entire way.

Sauté some aromatics—onion, celery, and carrots—in olive oil in a stockpot. When they are fragrant, add the chicken (3 ½ pounds [1.6 kg] is a good size) to the pot and cover with cool water. Add a handful of black peppercorns if you have them. Bring up over medium-high heat and skim the scum as it bubbles off. Once it's all clean, put a lid on it, turn the burner off, and let sit for half an hour. Pull at the drumstick with tongs. If it gives way, pull the chicken out and cool. Pick out the bones and add them back to the stockpot to simmer for an hour and a half. You never want to boil stock—it takes too much from the chicken bones in an unsavory manner and breaks down the fat into the stock so you can't skim it. This way of cooking ensures its moisture and gives you stock at the same time. You need this stock to make the sauce for the pot pie, so you've almost literally killed two birds with one stone. The chicken is juicy and can handle some more cooking, since it's almost like it brined in the stockpot a bit.

Cooking Seafood

Seafood is the one protein that can and should go in a pie raw. It cooks along with the baking crust. Raw oysters and various types of whitefish are great in seafood pies. When you pick the oysters pick big ones, and always keep their liquor, as that enhances the flavor. The meat of a poached oyster is more apparent and is more fond of a pot pie, rather than, say, a small oyster. Save the small one for the raw bar.

It's odd to me to use lobster in a pie. The lobster must be cooked, or at least par-cooked before it is in the pie. I can't imagine shelling a live lobster for its meat. When a lobster cooks too long, the meat becomes rubbery. Lobsters are pretty expensive. Certainly it can be made to be tasty, all of it together—that's what butter and wine are for. It's just not the best way to eat a lobster, so let's leave it at that.

Tomato Pie

Saltine Crust

1 stick (½ cup) (112 g) unsalted butter, melted

1 sleeve crackers or 1 ¾ cups (205 g) cracker crumbs

1 egg white

Mayonnaise

1 clove fresh garlic

1 tablespoon (15 g) mustard

2 whole eggs and 1 yolk

1 cup (235 ml) light olive or canola oil

zest and juice of 1 lemon

1 teaspoon (5 ml) vinegar, ideally sherry, apple cider, or white wine

1 teaspoon (6 g) kosher salt

Tomatoes

1 pound (455 g) of whole cherry, grape, or Sun Gold tomatoes

When I put the word out for recipes, Harry Rosenblum, who owns the Brooklyn Kitchen with his wife Taylor Erkkinen, told me he'd look for his tomato pie recipe. I've never had tomato pie, but I was intrigued, until I came across the name of a classic prepackaged baking mix in the recipe. I don't know why it turned me off so much—there must be some sort of childhood trauma I've managed to repress over the years. Let's let sleeping dogs lie in that category, and just be happy that recipe inspired this one.

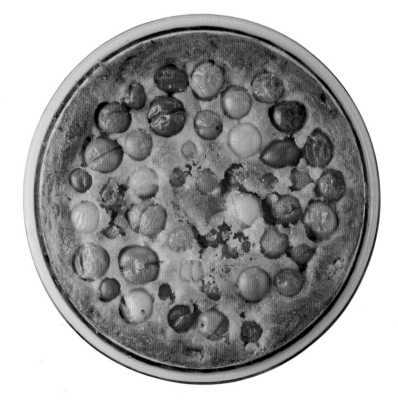

Originally I tried to do a Cheddar-cheese cracker crust for this pie, but it was just too much. Tomato pie classically has Cheddar cheese with it, and rarely do I want to violate a Southern recipe. I thought by using the Cheddar crackers I was incorporating the cheese in a clever manner. Sometimes cleverness and food do not mix, and this is one of them. I settled on the less-showy, more delicious saltine crust and omitted the cheese. It's important to keep the integrity of the cracker crust dry, so I changed the blanched and sliced tomatoes to Sun Gold tomatoes whole. I love whole tiny tomatoes—they just pop in your mouth.

Finally I changed the canned mayonnaise to homemade mayonnaise. The mayonnaise gives the pie amazing flavor, but also the structure. All said and done, this is a pretty easy pie to make.

Preheat the oven to 375°F (190°C, gas mark 5).

Saltine Crust

Melt your butter in a saucepan and let it cool a bit. Put your sleeve of crackers in the food processor and let it roll for a bit. You don't want the crumb to be like dust. With the food processor on add the melted butter in a stream and then the egg white. The egg white adds a nice cohesion to the crust. Press the mixture in a pie plate and form the crust up the sides. It will be ¼-inch (6 mm) thick. Refrigerate the crust for 15 minutes before baking.

Place in the preheated oven. Pull out after 15 minutes.

Mayonnaise

You can make this mayonnaise in a blender or by hand in a bowl, but probably not your food processor because the standard size of a food processor needs more eggs in it to catch on the blade. There is nothing sadder than the moment your mayonnaise or aioli did not work. Then thankfully that moment passes.

If making by hand, mince your clove of garlic and put it in a bowl with the mustard, eggs, and egg yolk. Place the bowl on a kitchen towel so it stays put. Whisk the garlic, eggs, and mustard together. Pour the oil in a liquid measuring cup with a spout for pouring. Add the oil in a small, steady stream to the bowl, whisking the entire time. The bowl should be stable on the towel. It's paramount to add the oil in a slow stream, especially in the beginning, so it becomes incorporated into the eggs, otherwise it won't work. This is called emulsifying. Whisk in the zest and juice of the lemon, vinegar, and salt. Taste for more acid or salt.

Yield: 1 ½ cups (340 g) mayonnaise

Assemble

Turn your oven up to 400°F (200°C, gas mark 6).

Pick through your tomatoes for duds and stems. Put in a single layer on top of the saltine crust. Pour the mayonnaise evenly over the tomatoes. It should almost be level with the sides of the pie plate if it's a 9-inch (23 cm) plate. It's fine if it is above the edges of the crust. Place in the oven for 20 minutes. The pie is done when the mayonnaise sets up and gets a little brown on top. The pie is set when you gently shake it and it only jiggles in the very center.

Pull and let cool for 30 minutes.

Optional: Finish with fresh herbs such as basil or chives.

Yield: 1 pie (8 servings)

Oyster Pie

Oysters are a serious gift in this world. They are one of my favorite foods, something I have been eating my entire life either raw or cooked. Oysters pack a lot of flavor, the meat and the liquid together, so it's important to utilize both.

You truly get what you pay for regarding seafood. There is no other food like seafood that will so readily indicate whether it should be eaten. There is rarely a middle ground with fish or mollusks; rarely a point when you wonder, "Hmm, I'm not sure if this is good." It's called instinct for a reason. You smell something bad, it is bad. That's how the food world works—especially seafood.

Mollusks are alive while you are keeping them, so they must be stored correctly, in a very cold refrigerator (not freezing) and not sitting in water. Oysters are fairly resistant and can last for up to a week if stored well. The heft of an oyster is a fantastic indicator of its state: Comparatively a heavier one is fresher, as its weight includes the shell, oyster, and liquid. Oysters are similar to eggs in that way—the heavier ones are better, but you cannot tell what's going on inside until you crack it open.

- -

I am from Maryland, which has a wealth of food history pertaining to oysters. I grew up eating raw oysters and oyster stuffing every year at the holidays. The old recipes, also known as "receipts," opened my eyes to my mother's side of the family, generations native to Maryland. What we ate growing up on my grandfather's farm, what he valued, was the fresh food he grew himself, and crabs and oysters. I love reading the ancient recipes, because these ladies were mainly concerned with not overcooking the oysters. They prebake all the crusts and then cook the oysters in a pan and pour them in the pie.

- -

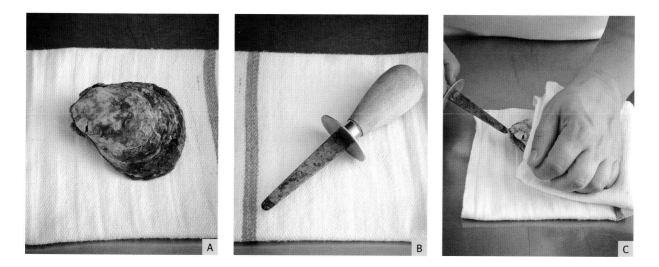

Choosing and Shucking Oysters

Consider the weather when you purchase oysters: Where is it hot? Avoid it. An old saying goes to only buy oysters in the months ending in r, the idea being that they're not good in the warmer months May, June, July, and August. Luckily we have refrigeration since that notion took hold. If it's hot where I am, I look to the waters farther north for oysters.

When you buy oysters, ask your fishmonger what is good. It's always a good idea to cultivate relationships with the people from whom you purchase food; they know what's really going on. They are also great people to discuss food in general with; not only what looks good at the moment but what is appropriate for what you are making.

In general I prefer small oysters raw and to use bigger oysters for baking, smoking, or frying. A big oyster raw is a bit unseemly for me, but it's quite versatile cooked. It's a pity to use lovely small fresh oysters to cook, because they want to be eaten raw. Bigger oysters can be shucked and cut up and really stretch a bit more in a cooked method. They end up being a better value.

Another important thing your fishmonger can tell you is which oysters are the easiest to shuck. Consider this welcome information, not only because it makes your life easier, but also cuts down on the waste from frustrating oysters that just won't open.

Buy an oyster knife. The blade should flex, but not be too flexible, and have a slight tilt at the end. Beware of oyster knives that look like shivs. One slip from an oyster knife and it ends up in your palm. One slip from an uncharacteristically sharp oyster knife and it ends up through your palm.

To shuck an oyster: Clean your oysters; they're dirty. There is a point of an oyster where you open it in the shallow top that has a hinge at the most narrow point where the two shells meet. This is where you will put your oyster knife and open it, so scrub that area of the shell. Mud tends to sit there because it is a rivet.

Next, place the oyster on a folded-up kitchen towel. Its use is twofold: a steady surface to work on and a safety for your nondominant hand against the oyster knife lest it slips (a, b). The hinge of the oyster should be facing your dominant hand with the oyster knife in it. Fold the towel on top of the body of the oyster (c).

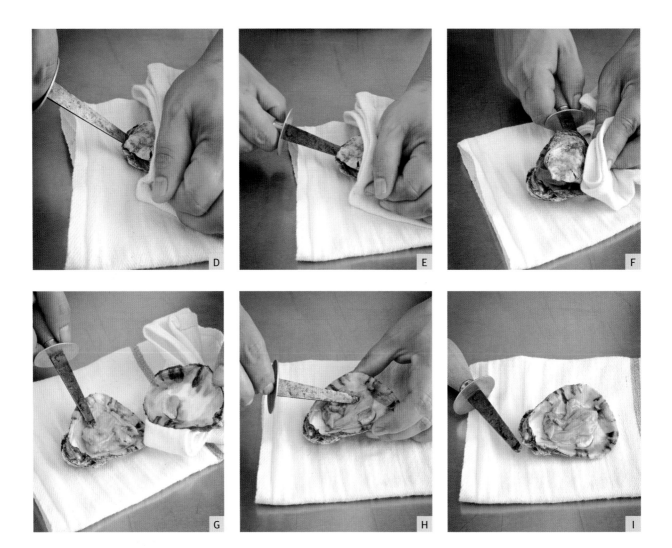

Take the end of the oyster knife and gently wedge it into the hinge of the oyster, somewhere between a 30-degree angle and a 45-degree angle (d). If you slowly move it in the hinge itself will designate the angle—you're just easing the knife in until it has enough leverage to crack the shell open (e). Continue moving it in until you have to give the flick of force to open it, as you will just wedge the knife in until it has to make the move. Open the shell by turning the knife and then moving it across the top part of the shell to completely open the shell and sever the oyster from the top shell (f). Then put the knife at the bottom of the shell where the oyster is attached and flip it, extracting it from the foot (g, h). Keep all the liquid. It is important (i).

Smell the oyster. Does it smell like the ocean or like ammonia? Look at it. Is there liquid in the shell or is it dry? If any seafood ever smells like ammonia, throw it out, because it has turned. Also throw out any oysters that are dry. You get what you pay for. The payback from your body for bad seafood is pretty vicious.

As with everything, you learn by doing. So always offer yourself as the oyster shucker.

Making Oyster Pie

I like to prepare these in individual bowls topped with prebaked crusts. Then the precious oysters don't overcook and you cut down on the prep time.

Preheat the oven to 425°F (220°C, gas mark 7).

Bottom Crust

Roll out your crusts to ¼-inch (6 mm) thick. Use the rim of a small bowl as a template and cut the top crust out. Put them on baking sheets, brush with the egg and bake for 20 to 25 minutes or until they are golden brown. Pull out of the oven and keep warm on the baking sheet.

Filling

In a large cast iron or Dutch oven over medium heat melt the butter and add the onions. When they soften, add the flour in and whisk well for a roux. Add the celery and potatoes. Cook until almost soft, then add the heavy cream and white wine; keep whisking. You want the raw wine flavor to come out and for the sauce to thicken to a gravy; about 15 minutes. Season with salt, pepper, mace, nutmeg, and hot sauce. Taste.

Shuck the oysters and reserve the liquid. If the oysters are larger than 2 inches (5 cm) long, cut them in half. If they can remain whole do so. Add the oysters, their liquor, and the peas to the sauce and cook on a low simmer for about 5 minutes. They are done when the edges curl a bit and the middle is a bit firm.

At the last moment roll your flat parsley in a tight bundle and give a good chop. Thinly slice the fresh chives. Add the herbs, along with the finish of lemon zest and juice to the filling. Pour the filling into bowls and top with the crust tops. Eat.

Yield: 6 servings

Crust
Basic Pie Crust (page 18), chilled

Filling
5 tablespoons (70 g) unsalted butter
2 onions, small dice
24 oysters in the shell
3 tablespoons(24 g) all-purpose flour
2 celery stalks, small dice
2 medium-size potatoes, medium dice (optional)*
1½ cups (355 ml) heavy cream
¼ cup (60 ml) white wine
   salt to taste
   freshly ground black pepper
¼ teaspoon mace
¼ teaspoon freshly grated nutmeg
   jigger of hot sauce
1 cup (150 g) fresh peas
   bunch of flat parsley
   bunch of chives
   zest and juice of 1 lemon

Wash
1 lightly beaten egg

I make the potatoes optional because maybe you don't want their starchiness. With them, I feel like this references a chowder. You make the call.

Oysters and Sweetbread Pie

Crust

Basic Pie Crust (page 18), chilled

Filling

1 pound (455 g) sweetbreads

2 cups (475 ml) milk (optional)

salt for soaking

4 large ears of corn, yields 2 cups (300 g)

2 medium-size zucchini

1 large shallot

8 to 12 oysters, depending on size, with their liquor

¼ cup (60 ml) dry white wine

2 tablespoons (16 g) all-purpose flour

1 cup (235 ml) heavy cream

2 tablespoons (28 g) unsalted butter

zest and juice of 1 lemon

1 teaspoon (6 g) kosher salt

½ teaspoon (3 g) freshly ground black pepper

3 tablespoons (12 g) chopped fresh chives or parsley (optional)

Wash

1 beaten egg or 4 tablespoons (60 ml) milk

sea salt

Look for larger oysters for this recipe, or buy a pint of shucked oysters in their liquid. I make this in ramekins or small crocks—a big slice of pie is a bit too much. A little of this goes a long way, so these are quite potent individual servings.

Sweetbreads commonly refer to the thymus or pancreas gland of usually a calf or lamb. When correctly cooked they are sweet and soft, so this combination with oysters makes sense, since they are also meaty, sweet, and soft.

Instead of going the classic pot pie really rich route, I use corn and zucchini in this pie—they are a light and sunny addition.

Ramekins are great for this; they are ceramic single-serving bowls that can handle the heat of the oven and give a great shape to a pot pie. If possible, use 8-ounce ones. If necessary, 4-ounce will suffice.

ANYTHING THAT IS FROM DEEP INSIDE AN ANIMAL, AN ORGAN OR GLAND, SHOULD BE CLEANED FOR BEST FLAVOR AND TEXTURE.

Four hours before preparing the pie:

Clean the Sweetbreads

Cover the sweetbreads with milk and 1 teaspoon salt and let sit for at least 3 hours. The milk helps to leach out the impurities. Drain as needed and refill. The longer they sit, the better it is.

Bring a medium-size pot of salted water up to boil. Squeeze half a lemon in it. Pull out the sweetbread and rinse. Prepare an ice bath close by. Turn the water down to a simmer and slip the sweetbread in for about 2 minutes. It will become more opaque and a bit firm. Pull it out and put it in the ice bath. Pull the outer membrane from the nodules. It may seem quite thick—membranes usually are. It will pull off together and leave you with the naked glands, which are different sizes depending on what kind of sweetbreads they are. Cut the sweetbreads into pieces no smaller than ¼ inch (6 mm).

Preheat the oven to 425°F (220°C, gas mark 7). Put a baking sheet in the oven to preheat also.

Crust

Cut 1 chilled pie crust into quarters and roll into spheres. Refrigerate three while you roll out one to ⅛-inch (3 mm) thick. Line a ramekin with the crust and trim to ¼ inch (6 mm) of overhang. Refrigerate prepared ramekins.

Filling

Shuck your corn and pick the silk out. Place a clean kitchen towel on your surface. Hold the cob by its natural handle and place the butt on the towel. With your sharpest knife, cut the kernels off the cob, starting at the top. Then take the straight side of a butter knife and shave the naked cob of all its milk. Put the corn in a bowl. Cut the zucchini into a small dice; they should be about the size of the corn kernels or a little larger. Mince your shallot.

Shuck your oysters and put them in a small bowl with their liquor. Make certain there are no shell fragments. If the oysters are quite large, chop them into pieces no smaller than ½ inch (1 cm). Add the white wine to the oysters and liquor.

Mix the vegetables, oysters, oyster liquid, and sweetbreads together in a bowl. Toss with the flour and heavy cream. Cut up the butter and mix it throughout. Season with the lemon juice and zest, salt, and pepper. Add chopped parsley or chives if you have it and season, if necessary.

Pull your other crust out of the refrigerator. Cut into quarters and roll each into spheres.

Get the pastry-lined ramekins out of the oven and fill with the filling. Top each ramekin with the rolled-out tops, trim, and crimp up. Cut slits into the top crust, brush with egg or milk, and sprinkle with sea salt.

Put the ramekins on the baking sheet and bake for about 30 or 40 minutes. These little pies are ready when the crust is golden brown.

Yield: 4 servings

Smoked Fish Pie

Top Crust

5 large Idaho potatoes

1 tablespoon (19 g) kosher salt

6 tablespoons (84 g) unsalted butter, softened

½ cup (120 ml) heavy cream

Filling

1 pound (455 g) smoked fish (trout, white, blue)

2 leeks

3 tablespoons (42 g) unsalted butter

3 tablespoons (45 ml) olive oil

1 cup (235 ml) white wine, champagne, or rosé dry, not sweet

1 cup (235 ml) stock, possibly 2 (475 ml)

2 teaspoons kosher salt

4 stalks celery with tender leaves

½ pound (225 g) mushrooms, ladies' choice

3 tablespoons (24 g) all-purpose flour

¾ cup (175 ml) heavy cream

2 tablespoons (14 g) bread crumbs

1 teaspoon (6 g) salt

1 teaspoon (6 g) freshly ground black pepper

1 cup (60 g) picked parsley leaves

zest and juice of 1 lemon

more butter to dot the top

I spent a fated day at the seaside in England at Whitstable, a beautiful place to sit on a wall and watch the vast sky disappear beneath the ocean. Along the way I tried a few of the famed English pies, and the one that really blew me away was a fish pie. In the world of seafood I am partial to shellfish. Fish sometimes lacks a presence.

Until you smoke it. Smoked fish is delicious, and for a little you get a lot. The smoked element of the fish delivers a lot of flavor, while the same fish, unsmoked in the pie, is really just a texture, a protein.

The crust is mashed potatoes, and the mashed potatoes are delicious. And don't worry about overcooking the fish; it's already cooked.

Top Crust

Peel your potatoes, cut them into same-size chunks, put them in a sauce pot, and cover with cold water. Add a tablespoon of kosher salt. Place over high heat. Bring to a boil and then just turn down a tiny bit so it's not boiling violently. Check the potatoes at 10 minutes. If you can pierce them with a butter knife, strain them out of the water. Put a bowl under the colander, take a stiff wooden spoon, and press the potatoes through the mesh. Add the softened butter in chunks and whisk in rapidly so the heat of the potatoes melts the butter. Add the heavy cream in a steady stream. Finish with kosher salt to taste. The potatoes should be creamy. Add more butter if they're not. Set aside.

Filling

Pick through your smoked fish for bones, but don't break the flesh down to tiny pieces. Try to keep big pieces so your pie has some guts to it. Cut the dark green ends off the leeks, save for stock, but keep the root attached. Slice down the leeks lengthwise to expose the innards. Try to keep the last outer skin on so it keeps its shape. Sometimes leeks are oppressively dirty, so take care to clean them. Expose the inner circle of the leek and rinse it under cool water. Then cut the leeks into ⅓-inch (8 mm) thickness. (If you suspect they are still dirty, put them in a bowl with cool water. Just make sure the water is much deeper than the leeks so gravity will take the dirt away. (Vegetables grow in dirt. They get dirty.) Melt 3 tablespoons (42 g) of unsalted butter and 3 tablespoons (45 ml) of olive oil in a cast iron. Add the leeks, and then a cup (235 ml) of white wine, rosé, or champagne and a cup (235 ml) of stock. Add a teaspoon of kosher salt. Bring up to a simmer and let the leeks simmer for about 20 minutes. You want them to get soft. Stalks like this need to simmer a bit to become more inviting to eat.

Clean the celery stalks, reserving the lightest-colored leaves. Cut the celery on the bias, at a slight angle, no thicker than ¼ inch (6 mm). You don't want it to be chunky, and you don't want it to be flimsy. You want it to have some body to it. Next, pop the stems off your mushrooms if you're using buttons or cremini. You do not need to spring for really fancy, expensive mushrooms; they're going in a pie full of cream and topped with mashed potatoes. Slice your mushrooms to the same thickness as the celery. Add the mushrooms to the leeks and stir them together. Let the mushrooms give a little bit. The mushrooms' flavor emerges during sautéing; they are quite porous, so they absorb the liquid and then they transform. Their depth reveals itself during the process. They turn from being more of texture, like a sponge, to an enhanced robust taste. They just need a bit of time and salt. Next add the celery and toss the mushrooms, celery, and leeks together. You really just want to introduce the celery to the pan, just to take the rawness out of it, about 5 minutes.

Add the flour to the pan. There should be liquid to absorb it; whisk it in until it is absorbed. Add ¾ cup (175 ml) cream in a steady stream so it is absorbed. Let this simmer for a few minutes so everything becomes friendly and integrated. Taste it. The flour should be cooked out, as should the alcohol of the wine. Add the bread crumbs to give the pie some body. This should be not very liquid, but a bit jiggly. Add the smoked fish and mix everything together. Salt and pepper to taste.

Roll the parsley leaves in a tight ball and give them a quick, coarse chop. Do the same with the celery leaves. Mix the parsley with no more than ¼-cup (15 g) chopped celery leaves. Zest the lemon and add it to the herbs, mixing them together. Juice the lemon into the trout-vegetable mixture. Pour the mixture into a pie plate and top with the herbs. Allow this to set for an hour, so it cools and firms up.

Add the mashed potatoes as a layer atop the smoked fish cream filling. Dot the mashed potatoes with butter and bake at 450°F (230°C, gas mark 8) for 10 or 15 minutes, until the top becomes golden and crisp.

Eat! This pie is also incredibly delicious cold.

Yield: 1 pie (8 servings)

Chicken Fat and Pea Pie

Crust

Basic Pie Crust (page 18), chilled

Filling

½ cup (100 g) chicken fat chopped roughly, not bigger than ½ inch (1 cm)

1 tablespoon (15 ml) olive oil

4 shallots, minced

3 cups (390 g) frozen green peas—yes, you can use fresh if you are in the moment ...

1 tablespoon (4 g) fresh tarragon

1 teaspoon minced mint—do not use spearmint or chocolate mint. It's nasty.

1 cup (235 ml) or so of chicken stock

salt and pepper

Food reveals a lot about us, and part of this is the specifics of where we live and what is happening. This pie has a definite backwoods quality to me, in the best way possible, utilizing chicken fat, both rendered and cracklings.

This pie looks to satisfy what months of winter can do to you. English peas freeze and keep well in freezer bags. For this pie, it is acceptable to use frozen peas. It's the dead of winter—what else are you going to do?

- - - - - - - - - - - - - - - - - - - -

I have never spent a winter in Maine, where Ladleah Dunn, who shared this recipe, lives. If there was ever a chance of that happening, the following words from Ladleah erased that compulsion:

"Adapted from a John Thorne recipe—we both spent time in hideous little cold cabins in Castine, Maine, thirty years apart. Inspired to cook the same foods. Chicken fat—the unsung crisp."

- - - - - - - - - - - - - - - - - - - -

Preheat the oven to 425°F (220°C, gas mark 7).

Bottom Crust

Roll out your chilled bottom crust to ⅛-inch (3 mm) thick and about 13 inches (33 cm) in diameter. Place in your pie pan per the instructions in chapter 3. Trim the edges so there is no more than ¼ inch (6 mm) of overhang. Lift and crimp the overhang along the rim. Chill in the refrigerator or freezer.

Filling

Render the chicken fat in a skim of oil till crispy and golden in a cast iron over low heat. Get as much fat from the skin as possible so cracklings are crispy. Take out and reserve.

Sauté shallots in the fat from the chicken rendering until translucent, about 7 minutes. Add these to the crispy chicken fat along with about a tablespoon of the hot rendered fat.

Pour in the peas. Toss in hot fat, and then with a slotted utensil remove the peas to the bowl with the fat and shallots. Toss with herbs and seasonings.

With remaining fat (add a wodge of butter if necessary) make a loose roux (see page 146), with flour and add stock to make a gravy. Adding chopped giblets is optional. Season to taste.

Fill bottom shell with pea/fat mixture. Add gravy till just wet. Place the top crust over the pie. Bake until golden and bubbly, about 50 minutes

Yield: 1 pie (8 servings)

Lamb Neck Pie

Braising the Lamb

lamb neck or shoulder (2.5 or 3 pounds)
(1 or 1.5 kg)

2 tablespoons (30 ml) olive oil

kosher salt

freshly ground black pepper

1 tablespoon (7 g) sumac

3 tablespoons (60 g) pomegranate
molasses

5 cloves garlic, smashed

1 large onion, medium dice

fennel tops without the fronds,
medium dice

3 stalks celery, medium dice

2 carrots, medium dice

2 cups (480 g) canned tomatoes,
crushed with your hands

2 cups (475 ml) stock

2 cups (475 ml) red wine

bunch of parsley

Chickpeas

2 cups (500 g) dried beans soaked
overnight

3 garlic cloves

¼ cup (60 ml) olive oil

Pot for braising

stockpot or Dutch oven

When I think of lamb I think of my Yia Yia Aritee Souris, who emigrated to the U.S. from Greece and opened a bar and restaurant when Prohibition ended; Paula Wolfert, whose cookbooks on Mediterranean food have influenced my life; and Tamara Reynolds, a friend who can roast a lamb leg like an old Greek lady.

Paula Wolfert's cookbooks offer incredible insight to how people really eat. She always goes straight to the source in her travels: the home kitchen. My Yia Yia used to cook Greek food all day long. Never an Easter passed without the requisite lamb with mint jelly. No one in my world recently has made more lamb that I know of than Tamara Reynolds. She made up a rub for her lamb leg that uses pomegranate molasses and Aleppo pepper. I also use sumac in the braise. Aleppo has a bit of heat and fruit to it while sumac is a bit acidic. Both are wondrous.

Braising the Lamb

Bring your lamb up to room temperature, out of the refrigerator for at least 45 minutes. Heat the olive oil in the Dutch oven over a medium-high flame. Season the lamb liberally with kosher salt, freshly ground pepper, sumac, and pomegranate molasses. When the olive oil starts to smoke a bit, or the flick of flour dances in it, place the lamb in the pot. Turn the lamb once this part of it is browned, about 3 minutes. Continue to brown the lamb on all sides and ends. The flame should be still medium high or a touch more, but if it's cranked the oil will most likely burn. Take the lamb out. If the oil smells burned, carefully pour it out into a glass measuring cup, wipe it clean, put the Dutch oven back on the burner, and add more oil.

Toss the smashed garlic cloves in and stir. When the garlic becomes fragrant, add the onions and let them hang together for a few minutes. Add the rest of the vegetables. Don't burn the garlic. It's not okay. There are worse things in this world, they are: famine, poverty, politicians, burned garlic. Vigilance is key.

Sauté the braise vegetables until fragrant. Add the crushed tomatoes, stock, and wine. Let it mingle for a bit and then add the lamb. Cover and keep over medium-low heat for 5 hours, or until the meat easily pulls off the bone. Pull the lamb out, let cool, and pick the bones. Strain the braising liquid. Take a wooden spoon or spatula and press all the liquid out of the braising solids. There is a lot of flavor in these vegetables—don't let it all end up in the bin.

Cool the liquid and take off the fat on top of it. Discard the fat. There is a reason why you don't really hear a lot about lamb fat. It is not a delicious fat.

This yields about 3 cups (675 g) of meat. Pour some braising liquid over it so it doesn't dry out.

Preparing the Chickpeas

While you are braising the lamb, cook some chickpeas. They're a great addition to this pie as a starch. Feel free to use canned chickpeas. I am touched by the difference when dried chickpeas are used, so for me it's worth it to use them. Anytime you buy dried beans you have to sort through them for rocks and bad beans. Nothing ruins a meal faster than biting down on a rock.

Dried beans are really hard. It's best to soak them overnight. Put them in a stockpot and fill it with water. Cover and leave out overnight. The beans absorb a lot of water and will cook faster and better for soaking. Drain and rinse the beans with cool water, put in a clean stockpot, and cover with cool water, about 5 inches (13 cm) above the beans. Smash a few cloves of garlic and put ¼ cup (60 ml) of olive oil in the water. Bring to a boil over a high flame, skim the scum, and let it continue to simmer. Add more water if necessary. Do not salt the water until the end or the beans will never really give. For beans to be their best they need to be creamy. Check the beans. When they are soft, add salt for flavor. Turn off and let sit in the liquid.

(continued)

Putting the Lamb Pie Together

(continued from page 141)

Crust

Basic Pie Crust (page 18), chilled

Sauce

3 tablespoons (42 g) unsalted butter

3 tablespoons (24 g) all-purpose flour

2 ½ cups (595 ml) lamb braising liquid

1 cup (235 ml) chickpea cooking liquid

½ cup (120 ml) red wine (optional)

Filling

1 white onion, medium dice

2 tablespoons (28 ml) olive oil

2 heads of fennel

1½ cup (50 g) large green olives, pitted

3 cups (675 g) pulled braised lamb

3 cups (492 g) cooked chickpeas

2 teaspoons (12 g) kosher salt

2 teaspoons freshly ground black pepper

1 tablespoon (6 g) Aleppo pepper

1 teaspoon (6 g) freshly grated nutmeg

⅛ teaspoon freshly grated cinnamon

zest and juice of 1 lemon

bunch of mint

deep 9 ½-inch (24 cm) glass pie plate
or 9-inch (23 cm) cast-iron pan

pie bird (optional)

All of these ingredients together make sense in a loose Mediterranean way, a variation on a tagine with lamb, tomatoes, olives, chickpeas, and fennel. Harmony in a pie crust. When you use such richly braised meat, it's great to end with something fresh, and nothing says fresh like lemon zest and mint.

Sauce

Melt the butter in your Dutch oven over medium heat and add the flour. Whisk together and let the flour cook out a bit, about 5 minutes. Add in a stream the braising liquid, whisking the whole time, and then add the chickpea liquid. Add the ½ cup (120 ml) of red wine if you want. The sauce will thicken quickly. It is the ideal viscosity when it coats the spoon or spatula. Turn the heat off under the sauce.

Filling

Cut and peel the onion. Heat 2 tablespoons (28 ml) of olive oil in a sauté pan and sauté the onion until fragrant and translucent. Cut your fennel heads in half, core them, and then slice along the grain in strips no thicker than ¼ inch (6 mm). Add to the pan and toss. Cook for a few minutes so the fennel gives a bit and loses its crunch. Smash the olives with the side of your knife. Pull them away from their pits.

Mix together the lamb, chickpeas, onions, olives, and fennel with the sauce and season. Taste. Season with salt, freshly ground black pepper, Aleppo pepper, nutmeg, cinnamon, and the zest and juice of 1 lemon. Taste again. Season as necessary.

You can make 1 whole pie, use a cast iron, or make individual pot pies. To make individual pot pies you can use ramekins, ovenproof bowls, or tiny cast irons. You have a choice here.

Constructing the Pie

Preheat the oven to 425°F (220°C, gas mark 7).

Roll out your chilled bottom crust to ⅛-inch (3 mm) thick. It should be about 13 inches (33 cm) in diameter. Place in your pie plate or cast iron per the instructions in chapter 3. Trim the edges so there is no more than ¼ inch (6 mm) of overhang. Lift and crimp the overhang along the rim of the pie pan. Chill bottom crust in the refrigerator or freezer.

Chop up a bunch of parsley leaves and mix it in the chilled filling. Pull out the chilled top crust from the refrigerator and roll out in the same manner and thickness. Get the pie plate or cast iron out of the refrigerator. If using a pie bird, place it, beak up, in the middle of the bottom crust and spoon the filling in around it. If not using a pie bird, put the filling in the crust. Place the filled pie pan adjacent to the top crust and treat it the same way, quickly flip it in half, and lift on top of the pie. Lift the other half over the pie. If there is a pie bird, just punch its beak through the top crust to vent. Lift the edges of the top crust up so the crust sits on top of the filling, not just stretched across it.

Trim the edges flush with the bottom crust and crimp them together. Cut slits in the top crust even if you do use a pie bird, brush the top crust with the wash, and sprinkle it with sea salt. Bake the pie at 425°F (220°C, gas mark 7) until the crust is golden brown. Pull and cool for at least half an hour. Finish with chopped mint.

Yield: 1 pie (8 servings)

Frito Pie

Chili

3 ½ pounds (1.6 kg) beef short rib on the bone (2 pounds [910 g] off the bone)

1 tablespoon (6 g) whole peppercorns

1 bay leaf

salt to taste

black pepper to taste

¼ cup (50 g) bacon fat

1 small onion, minced

1 large clove garlic, minced

2 teaspoons (5 g) whole cumin

¼ teaspoon allspice

3 whole cloves, crushed

1 teaspoon (2.3 g) cinnamon

2 teaspoons (3.5 g) cayenne pepper

½ cup (120 ml) coffee

12 ounces (355 ml) dark beer

2 cups (475 ml) beef broth

1 can (7 ounces) chipotle in adobo

½ tablet (2 oz [55 g]) Mexican chocolate

½ cup (63 g) masa harina

Topping

4 small bags of corn chips (1.25 ounces each)

Colby or yellow Cheddar cheese, grated for garnish

yellow onion, diced for garnish

Julie Farias is an astonishing whirling dervish of a chef, incredibly skilled in all aspects of the kitchen and most importantly in making delicious food. She grew up getting Frito pie from food trucks at the ball fields in San Antonio, Texas. I've never eaten anything like this out of a snack chip bag before getting this recipe.

This pie cuts to the heart of what savory pies are in the most basic right: portable food that won't dirty your hands. It's lunch or dinner with no cleanup.

This recipe calls for short rib meat that is excellent for long cooking, since it doesn't dry out. Short ribs can stand up to a lot of flavor. The corn chips make an excellent bottom crust; they don't get soggy and are a hearty complement to the meat.

1 Once the chili is made, open the bags of corn chips and cover halfway with it.

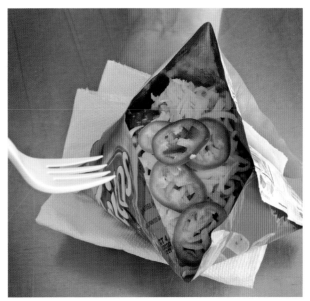

2 Add grated Colby or Cheddar cheese, diced onion, and slivered jalapeño, if you are so moved.

This recipe introduces bacon fat into your pies. When you fry bacon, save the fat. It keeps for a long time in your refrigerator, or you can freeze it. Bacon fat is perfect for this recipe. The nuance of its flavor to the onions is just another layer of taste for this pie.

Cut your short rib meat into ½-inch (1 cm) pieces. If you get it on the bone, by all means make stock. Cut the meat off the bones and roast the bones in an oven at 450°F (230°C, gas mark 8) until they are browned, about 20 minutes. Put the bones in a stockpot with a *mirepoix* (see page 122), and cover with cold water. Add a tablespoon of whole peppercorns and a bay leaf. Over high heat bring to a boil and skim the scum from the top of the stock. Lower the temperature to medium low and let the stock lightly simmer for at least 3 hours. Strain and reserve.

Season the diced meat with salt and pepper. Put the bacon fat in a Dutch oven or stockpot over medium heat, allowing it to melt. Add the short rib meat to brown. After about 3 minutes add your onion and garlic. Turn the heat down to medium and sweat them until they are translucent, about 5 minutes.

Toast your cumin seeds whole, and add to the meat and onions, along with the allspice, cloves, cinnamon, and cayenne. Mix well. Add the coffee, beer, and beef broth next, along with the chipotle. Stir everything together and bring it to a boil for a moment. Turn the pot down to a simmer and cook for about 5 hours.

Add the chocolate next. Chop a bit to help it dissolve in the pot. Mexican table chocolate packs a lot of flavor. Use half of a tablet.

Masa harina is a corn-based flour used in tamales and as a thickener. Put the ½ cup (63 g) of masa harina in a bowl and add two ladles of the braising liquid whisking together. Whisk well until the masa harina is smooth. Add to the chili in a steady stream and let everything simmer for at least 15 minutes. Taste for salt and pepper.

Yield: 4 servings

Chicken Pot Pie

Crust
Basic Pie Crust (page 18), chilled

Filling
4 tablespoons (60 ml) fat or olive oil

3 onions, large dice

½ bunch celery, large dice

4 medium-size carrots, large dice

2 cups (300 g) English peas

1 cup (110 g) potatoes, large dice (optional)

3 cups (420 g) shredded chicken

   gravy

Wash
1 lightly beaten egg or 3 tablespoons (45 ml) heavy cream

1 tablespoon (19 g) sea salt

   deep 9 ½-inch (24 cm) glass pie plate or 9-inch (23 cm) cast iron pan

   pie bird (optional)

Chicken pot pie: synonymous with love for many, or just eating your feelings. It is iconic. Read this entire recipe from start to finish. You need to understand what you are getting into.

These pies are not difficult, but it is imperative to accomplish more than one thing at a time. For this recipe, you must cook the chicken before it goes in the pie. You also cook the vegetables and make the gravy. Organize your tasks well and you can accomplish these things at the same time. If you only do one thing at a time in the kitchen, you'll never get anything done.

This sauce is very important for chicken pot pie. Don't even try to do it without.

A roux is a thickener that is equal parts fat and flour. This fat can be unsalted butter, chicken schmaltz, or bacon renderings. As food becomes more expensive, it is great to be able to use more and more by-products from what we make. You're not just cooking the chicken for pot pie, you are making stock from its bones that will then be used for the sauce for the pie, and the fat skimmed from the top of the stock can be used for the roux for the gravy. Or you can use bacon grease. The fat influences the flavor of the sauce.

There are different kinds of roux, and for this one you want to get it a dirty blonde color. The longer a roux cooks the darker it gets and the more impact it has on the food. The point of this roux is to provide thickening and a bit of depth.

The other things you need to make this sauce are stock, white wine, and heavy cream or milk. The stock is the main liquid, and the cream and wine complement with their own flavors and textures. The same ratio employed for a *mirepoix* (onion: 2 to carrot: 1 and celery: 1) works here (stock: 2 to cream: 1 and wine: 1). You can use any stock, but for the sake of chicken use chicken stock. The best pot for this is a Dutch oven or a big, somewhat deep cast iron. A roux really needs cast iron to cook well since it is so viscous.

Roux

 6 tablespoons (75 g) fat

 6 tablespoons (50 g) all-purpose flour

 ¾ cup (175 ml) heavy cream or milk, room temperature

 ¾ cup (175 ml) white wine, room temperature

 2 cups (475 ml) stock, room temperature

Place your cast iron over medium heat and put the fat in. As it melts, whisk the flour in batches so it can be incorporated into the fat as you go. This helps to cut down on the whisking lumps out on the back end. Keep whisking the roux as it is mixed. If it bubbles a bit too much, turn the flame down. A roux is a thick entity that can burn easily. Keep whisking the roux. Turn it on low. Even though the flour is mixed in with the fat it is still separate, so the roux has to keep on cooking to get the flour flavor out.

There is a rawness of the flour that you can smell and taste, but beware, because hot roux is a burning affair. To understand when the flour cooks out and this concoction becomes a roux takes practice. Luckily this regards a roux, which is commonplace in cooking, so there should be ample moments to learn this. The entire cooking time for this roux is about 10 minutes.

Add the room-temperature stock to the roux. Always add in a slow, steady stream to a roux while whisking; it cuts down on clumping and ensures that the liquid is absorbed. Next add the white wine and heavy cream in the same manner. Whisk everything together and let it set for a bit, whisking every now and again. The gravy should be over a medium heat, or even a bit higher if you are attending to it. It needs to reduce, and the disparate flavors need to cook together. If you can still taste the separate components of a sauce then it is still raw and needs to cooks longer. This gravy takes about 25 minutes to cook. To find the sweet spot between too runny and too thick: take your spatula or spoon out of the gravy and swipe your finger across it. The line you create should keep its shape and the sauce should be a delicate balance between translucent and opaque. Since it will cook and reduce a bit more in the pie, it is better to err on the side of a little thin rather than really thick. Season to taste. Gravy without salt and pepper is just a very loose, fat texture. It's not worth it.

Cooking the Chicken and Making the Stock

Chicken and Stock

2 tablespoons (28 ml) olive oil

1 onion, medium dice

4 pounds (1.8 kg) chicken, preferably air chilled

salt

3 stalks celery, medium dice

3 medium-size carrots, medium dice

water to cover

stems from a bunch of parsley
(the leaves will go in the pot pie)

sprig of fresh thyme

2 tablespoons (10 g) whole black peppercorns

Pot
stockpot

Just as there is a proper vessel for everything, there is a proper method in which to prepare chicken for a specific dish. Chicken is amazingly versatile; it can be roasted on high heat, deep-fried, pan-fried, braised, smoked, stewed, and even stuck on a beer can and put on a grill. Each way has its appropriate uses. For pot pie, if you have a whole chicken, put it in a pot with water. At the same time you are making stock for the gravy.

Heat the olive oil in a stockpot over medium-high heat and add the onions when it's hot. Stir it and when it just becomes fragrant, add the rest of the *mirepoix* (celery and carrots). Let it sauté for a few minutes. Salt the chicken inside and out and put in the stockpot. Cover with cold water and add the parsley stems, thyme, and peppercorns. The stock will begin to bubble after about 25 minutes. As this happens, a dirty foam will collect on the surface of the liquid. Get a ladle and discard it. You are now skimming the scum. Skim it all before it comes to a boil and reincorporates the scum into the stock. Cover the pot immediately with a lid and turn the burner off.

After 30 minutes check the chicken. Pull on the drumstick with tongs; it should be very wiggly. Pull the chicken out and let it cool until you can pick it. Take out the skin and bones, put back in the stockpot, and let it simmer for another hour. Shred your chicken into good pieces, not too chunky and nothing like cat food. Strain your stock and reserve 2 cups (475 ml) for gravy. Stock freezes really well or keeps in the refrigerator for up to 4 days.

The chicken is good and the stock is made. One 4-pound (1.8 kg) chicken yields 3 to 4 cups (675 to 900 g) of shredded meat, packed a bit.

The ratio of onions to carrots and celery should be even; this is a classic French *mirepoix*. It's used in stocks, soups, sauces, and braises. When you cut a *mirepoix* it's important for the vegetables to be the same size so they cook at the same time. These vegetables are an important part of the pot pie. They need to have some guts to counter the meat, so cut them in a large dice.

Heat 4 tablespoons (64 g) of butter, olive oil, or some other fat in a Dutch oven over medium heat. Add the onions and sauté them until translucent, about 10 minutes. The longer you cook onions the more they change, becoming sweeter and something completely different from their raw reality. Once they are soft and fragrant, add the celery, carrots, and peas. Mix together. Continue until they are just soft. Add the 3 cups (675 g) of the shredded chicken, mix together, and then add the gravy. Mix it all together and taste for seasoning. Salt? Freshly ground pepper? These two things separate food that is simple and all right from food that is simple and delicious. Let cool before putting into the pie crust.

Constructing the Pie

Preheat the oven to 425°F (220°C, gas mark 7).

Roll out your chilled bottom crust to ⅛-inch (3 mm) thick. It should be about 13 inches (33 cm) in diameter. Place in your pie plate or cast iron per the instructions in chapter 3. Trim the edges so there is no more than ¼ inch (6 mm) of overhang. Lift and crimp the overhang along the rim of the pie pan. Chill bottom crust in the refrigerator or freezer.

Chop up a bunch of parsley leaves and mix it in the chilled filling. Pull out the chilled top crust from the refrigerator and roll out in the same manner and thickness. Get the pie plate or cast iron out of the refrigerator. If using a pie bird, place it, beak up, in the middle of the bottom crust and spoon the filling in around it. If not using a pie bird, put the filling in the crust. Place the filled pie pan adjacent to the top crust and treat it the same way, quickly flip it in half, and lift on top of the pie. Lift the other half over the pie. If there is a pie bird, just punch its beak through the top crust to vent. Lift the edges of the top crust up so the crust sits on top of the filling, not just stretched across it.

Trim the edges to be flush with the bottom crust and crimp them together. Cut slits in the top crust even if you do use a pie bird, brush the top crust with the wash, and sprinkle it with sea salt. Put in the preheated oven and bake until golden brown, about 45 minutes.

Yield: 1 pie (8 servings)

Game Pie

Jim Harrison is an American writer who understands our appetites, for food, sex, drink, love, nature, and isolation better than anyone. His voice and ideas are places I really love to inhabit. He writes poetry, fiction, and pieces about food in a muscular manner that cuts through to the heart of the matter. His words are great companions. This "little note" from him is no exception. I contacted him to see if he had a recipe for game pie, because he is a hunter. We all need our ruses to get to our heroes. Mine worked.

This is also a great example of how people think of and relay recipes when they inhabit worlds like Harrison's. You can tell that he is comfortable in the kitchen, that he knows exactly what kind of stock is ideal for these pies, and that really, at the end of the day, whatever animal is hanging will be delicious in the lard crust. Herbs finish pies well, and wine even better.

"I don't have a recipe, but you could deduce one. I've made many game pies, which, when you think about it, are improbably valuable, because scarcely anyone hunts. This is probably worth less to you because no one has the ingredients. I make a stock out of veal bones or pork neck bones, to evolve the gelatin. In the spring or summer I take what's left of the fall and winter game, and pluck and roast it. It can be anything, like woodcock, ruffed grouse, doves, ducks, venison, antelope, Hungarian grouse, etc. I roast them only long enough to get the meat off the bones. The pieces are relatively small. I mix this with a judicious amount of the stock, and my wife has meanwhile made some lard crusts in pie tins. I give these as gifts but try to keep most for myself, to drink with a good Burgundy. Does this help? It's sort of English/French. I sometimes use marjoram or a dab of tarragon. There's a density of flavor there that gives you goosebumps.
Yrs., Jim"

He seems to think that his way is gone. Let's hope not.

Oxtail Pot Pie

Crust

Single Pie Crust (page 19), chilled

Braise

6 oxtails

kosher salt

freshly ground black pepper

2 onions

4 stalks celery

5 medium-size carrots

4 cloves garlic

6 tablespoons (90 ml) olive oil

3 cups (710 ml) stock
(chicken or beef is great)

3 cups (710 ml) red wine, beer,
or a mixture of both

Filling

4 cloves garlic

6 shallots, medium dice

2 tablespoons (28 ml) olive oil
or bacon fat

mixture of mildly hot and
sweet peppers, 6 total

2 tablespoons (28 g) unsalted butter

2 tablespoons (16 g) all-purpose flour

2 cups (475 ml) braising liquid from oxtail

3 medium green tomatoes, medium dice

kosher salt

fresh black pepper

2 teaspoons (5 g) smoked paprika

picked braised oxtail

Wash

1 lightly beaten egg

roux (optional)

I once worked at a restaurant where we made a really nice beef stock with oxtail. Oxtail is a beef cut that is just as it's called: the tail end of the cow. It is usually surrounded by a layer of fat, and the meat is embedded in the vertebrae. Oxtail is really a braising cut, but the luck of that is the longer something with all this fat and bone cooks, the more flavor it has. It's another great moment to set it and forget it with your Dutch oven, just checking in to make certain the braise is not going too low or too high. A simmer is ideal, where there are just a bit of bubbles at the top.

We used oxtail for a stock, but turned the rest of it over for a family meal once the stock was done. I braised it with whatever I could find for tacos or for pies. It is rich and a little goes a long way, so it can take a lot of flavor from its attending vegetables. When I braise red meat, I find it a good time to empty the wine bottles. Sometimes the wine in my house does not get drunk in a timely manner, that is, while the wine is still drinkable, which seems a pity. But it works well for a braise because I just empty the last bits of the bottle in the pot.

It is ideal for the liquid to be flush with the meat and vegetables. If you have too little liquid, your braise might be too thick, or burn. If you have too much liquid, your food might be engulfed. Make them even. If you must, use some water in addition to stock, wine, and/or beer. Everything you add to the pot should bring flavor. It's not just a liquid festival. But if you must, you may use water.

Season your oxtail with kosher salt and black pepper. Cut your onions, celery, and carrots to a medium dice. Keep your onions in a separate bowl. Lightly smash the garlic cloves with the side of your knife and keep with the onions. Heat your Dutch oven over a medium-high heat and then add 3 tablespoons (45 ml) olive oil. Once the oil shimmers a bit, add the oxtail to brown. It should sizzle. Make sure there is space between the oxtail as you brown it; meat likes space to brown. That means it is getting the attention from the heat that it needs. Leave at least 2 inches (5 cm) between the oxtails as you brown them. You probably need to do 2 batches of browning. Check the side down after 4 minutes. Is it a rich dark brown? If yes, turn over to brown the other side. If the color is more gray, then leave that side down until it is browned.

If the oil starts to smoke or get really dark brown, turn the flame down just a bit. You want it to be high so the pan is hot, and the meat should absorb the heat. Ideally, between the hot pan and the meat, an equilibrium is reached in temperature. If the meat does not sizzle when you place it in the pan, turn the pan up a bit. If the oil begins to get dark and continues to increase in temperature, turn the pan down.

Once browned, take the oxtail out of the pan. If the oil in the Dutch oven smells burned or is really dark, pour it out. If it smells burned, it is burned. This affects everything for the rest of the cooking process. Also, if there is a moment when your food is sticking to the bottom of your pan or pot and you suspect it might be burned, then change pots. You can save the food you are cooking by changing the vessels. When in doubt, switch the pots! When in doubt, pour off the fat and begin anew!

So disregard any burned meat bits in your pan and add 3 tablespoons (45 ml) of olive oil. Sauté the garlic and onions over a medium heat until you can smell them. Then add the carrots and celery. Once it is all fragrant and the vegetables begin to soften, add the oxtail, the stock, and the alcohol. Bring everything up to a boil and then turn down to a simmer. Let it cook for between 3 and 4 hours—when the meat begins to fall off the bone. Pull the oxtail and place on a baking sheet. Strain the braise through a colander. Press the solids to extract all of their flavor. Discard the solids. Let the braising liquid cool so you can take the fat off the top. The fat settles to the top of a stock or soup. If you cool it completely, it becomes solid and you can just pull it off.

Once cooled, pick the meat off the bone. The intricate system of meat on the oxtail; it wraps around and in the crevices of the bone. There is a layer in the thick outside layer of fat.

The oxtail, braised on the bone for hours, is a rich and densely flavored meat. Shallots are a fantastic complement. Their flavor is a variation between red onions and garlic. Because the meat is so rich, use a mixture of sweet and hot peppers. There are such a range of peppers beyond green peppers and jalapeños—I like a mixture of Italian and banana peppers. I use green tomatoes here for a nice addition.

Thinly slice the garlic lengthwise and cut the shallots medium dice. Heat the olive oil in a pan over medium heat and sauté the shallots. Cut and deseed the peppers to a medium dice and add to the shallots, sautéing until soft. Add the butter and let it melt and then slowly add the flour in to create a roux. If the braising liquid from the oxtail coats the back of a spoon, you don't need to make the roux—it is thick enough. If it runs off the spoon though, it needs a bit of thickening. If you are making a roux, (see page 148) let the flour cook out a bit and then add the braising liquid. Mix everything together, and then add the oxtail. Mix well. If should be like a stew.

Preheat the oven to 425°F (220°C, gas mark 7).

Roll out a single crust to no less than ⅛-inch (3 mm) thickness. Line an 8-inch (20 cm) cast iron pan with the pie crust, lifting the edges so it is flush with the pan. Do not trim the edges. Put the filling in the pie, then lift the rough edges of the crust over the filling. You don't have to trim them. This is just a variation on a theme. You can certainly do a top crust for this pie, but you can also rock it galette-style. Brush the crust with a wash and put it in the oven for at least 30 minutes. The pie is finished when the crust is golden and crispy.

Yield: 1 pie (8 servings)

Breakfast Hand Pie

Crust

Basic Pie Crust (page 18), chilled

Filling

1 ½ pounds (670 g) thinly sliced country ham

1 ½ cups (150 g) grated cheese of your choosing

9 eggs

1 tablespoon (18 g) sea salt

Wash

1 lightly beaten egg

I like to think of hand pies as the homemade equivalent of the frozen swill you find in the freezer case, without the super-processed microwavable disgust factor. The food can be really elaborate with many steps, or the food can be quite simple. This one is simple, and it is done when the crust is done.

This is a standard ham and cheese with an egg. There are some beautiful country hams out there, and if you find a favorite ham, buy it and have your butcher slice it very thinly, almost like prosciutto. Country ham can be used for myriad things. In lieu of access to such hams, just use whichever is your favorite cured pork.

A more softly boiled egg will have leeway for the yolk to cook a bit more in the crust. To boil the eggs bring a pot of salted water to a boil and put the eggs in with a spoon. Prepare an ice bath. A soft-boiled egg, one where the yolk is completely soft, comes out at 4 ½ minutes. An egg with a slightly more cooked yolk comes out at 7 minutes, a creamy yolk at 10 minutes, and a solid yolk at 12. True soft-boiled eggs are very difficult to peel; they are pretty delicate.

The fresher the egg the more difficult it is to peel because its volume is greatest when it is fresh. The white loses volume as it ages. So as you curse the difficult eggs, know they are delicious. To make peeling eggs easier take a tack and pierce the middle of the wider bottom before putting it in the boiling water. The ice bath stops the eggs from cooking and makes them easier to handle and peel.

The final component to this hand pie is cheese, glorious cheese. Cheddar is fantastic, provolone divine and pepper jack the best. Pick what you like.

Preheat the oven to 425°F (220°C, gas mark 7).

Filling

Tear apart the ham so it is in large shreds that are more bite size than whole pieces. Grate the cheese and boil and peel the eggs. Slice them in ½-inch (1 cm) rounds.

Crust

Have a baking sheet ready. Pull out one of your crusts and break it up into 3 separate balls. Roll each one out as you would a pie, as round as possible. Do the same with the other crust. You are creating an assembly line.

Assemble

Put equal parts of ham in the center top third of each crust. It should be ¼ pound (115 g) of ham for each. Now place the sliced egg on top of the ham, spreading it out. This recipe allows for an egg and a half for each hand pie. Salt the eggs just a bit. End with the cheese spread out on top. Each pie gets ¼ cup (25 g) of cheese. Leave at least ½ inch (1 cm) around the perimeter of the crust.

Dip your pastry brush in some water and moisten the edges.

Fold the bottom half over the filling, so the edges are flush. Lightly press the air out of the hand pie and seal the edges together. Trim with a knife or pasta cutter. Make sure they are sealed. Move to the baking sheet and brush with egg wash.

Bake for 30 minutes, or until the pastry is golden brown. Eat soon thereafter.

Yield: 6 hand pies

Hot Pepper Pork Hand Pies

Hand Pie Crust

2 ½ cups (310 g) all-purpose flour

¼ cup (50 g) granulated sugar

1 tablespoon (19 g) kosher salt

¼ cup (60 ml) apple cider vinegar

¾ cup (175 ml) ice water

11 ounces cold unsalted butter

Hot Pepper Pork Filling

When choosing pork butt, look for a piece with a significant amount of fat on it. The more fat on the pork, the more flavor the meat will have.

3 pound (1.3 kg) pork butt

3 tablespoons (57 g) kosher salt

1 tablespoon (6 g) freshly ground black pepper

1 ½ tablespoons (9 g) ground fennel seed

2 tablespoons (8 g) ground red-pepper flakes

8 each habanero peppers

2 sweet red peppers

1 green pepper

1 onion

2 cloves of garlic

2 tablespoons (28 ml) olive oil

Pot
Dutch oven

This recipe is easy; it just takes time. Whenever you see the words pulled pork think about 5 hours of time. All it takes is preparation. It's not like you are literally standing over a fire with a cut of pork stoking the flames for hours, turning the spit.

Turn your oven on, chop some vegetables, season the meat, and go. The pork can be prepared as far as two days in advance. When you slow cook cuts of meat with significant fat caps on one side, you want to always cook with the fat side up so all the fat melts into the meat, lending it not only taste but richness and moistness.

Measure the flour, sugar, and salt into a large metal bowl. Mix well using a pastry cutter. In another bowl mix the vinegar and ice water. Let sit.

Cube cold butter into ¼- to ½-inch (6 mm to 1 cm) pieces. Add all the butter into the flour mixture and toss gently. Using the pastry cutter, cut the butter into the flour mixture until it resembles cornmeal but still has pea-size pieces of butter.

Use a ¼-cup (60 ml) measure to measure out the vinegar-water mixture. Sprinkle ¼ cup (60 ml) at a time over the flour/butter mixture and toss with your hands. Add until the dough has some larger clumps but is still dry. To test if the dough is ready, gently squeeze it together, flattening it down and folding it together. It will be a bit crumbly, but the folding and flattening of the dough creates the flaky layers in the cooked crust.

Wrap the dough in plastic wrap and refrigerate for at least 2 hours, ideally overnight.

Preheat the oven to 200°F (93°C, gas mark 1).

Hot Pepper Pork Filling

Liberally season the pork with salt, pepper, fennel, and red pepper flakes on all sides. Score the fat side with a sharp knife. Place in the Dutch oven, fat cap facing up, and put into the preheated oven with the lid off. Cook for about 6 hours or until you can pierce the butt with a fork and it breaks gently. Once the pork is done, take it out of the oven and allow to rest, turning periodically so it cools. As you turn it, take 2 forks to break it apart so it can sit in the drippings and absorb them.

Deseed the habaneros using rubber gloves. Habaneros are incredibly spicy, and their residue will linger on your fingertips longer than you remember you touched them. Peel the red and green peppers and deseed. Slice all the peppers into thin strips called julienne. Cut your onion in half, and slice along the grain in the same manner. Slice your cloves of garlic lengthwise also. Sauté the garlic, onion, and peppers together in 2 tablespoons (28 ml) of olive oil over medium heat. Don't overcook them; you want the peppers to retain their integrity. This is about 10 or 15 minutes.

Remove the pork from the Dutch oven and break it apart further so there are not big chunks. They won't pack well in a hand pie. Combine the pork and peppers and check for seasoning. Don't be bashful. Cool to room temperature, cover, and put in the refrigerator. A hot filling in a cold crust is an unfortunate matter.

Assembly

Unwrap the cold dough and roll it out on a well-floured surface to ⅛-inch (3 mm) thick. Using a 4-inch (10 cm) circular mold; cut out 12 circles. You can bring the scraps together and reroll if need be. If the bits are too warm, put them in the freezer for 20 minutes and reroll.

Take ¼ cup (56 g) of the pork and pepper filling and place in the middle of half of the circles. Brush the top circle with water and press over the filling, pressing firmly on the edges. Use a fork to crimp the edge, sealing it. Refrigerate or freeze for at least 1 hour. They keep for up to 2 weeks in the freezer.

Baking the Hand Pies

Preheat the oven to 400°F (200°C, gas mark 6).

Brush the hand pies with lightly beaten egg and sprinkle with sea salt. Bake for 30 minutes, rotating the tray after 15 minutes. They should be a dark golden brown, and the flakiness of the crust will be evident.

Yield: 6 hand pies

Sophie Kamin and Nate Smith offer this recipe for delicious pulled pork hand pies. As a couple, she's brilliant at pastry and he's an amazing chef. I caught them at a perfect moment, before their restaurant opened and they were selling these hand pies around town.

I love the addition of apple cider vinegar in these hand pies, and I think it's great to add as many tried-and-true recipes as possible as everyone has their own way.

Meat Pies

Crust

Basic Pie Crust (page 18), chilled

Filling

2 tablespoons (28 ml) olive oil

1 medium white onion, small dice

1 pound (455 g) ground beef

2 fresh jalapeños, small dice

2 poblanos, small dice

½ cup (120 ml) stock of your choice, or light beer

1 tablespoon (15 ml) vinegary hot sauce (I like Cholula)

2 teaspoons (12 g) kosher salt

freshly ground black pepper

2 teaspoons (4 g) madras curry powder

½ cup (60 g) bread crumbs

1 teaspoon (0.8 g) fresh thyme leaves

zest and juice of 1 lime

Wash

1 egg

These are the simplest thing to make. Meat pies use ground beef, but really you could use any ground meat you like or a combination of them. The important part of meat pies is to use ground meat with a significant percentage of fat. The same kind of grind you use for hamburgers or meatballs is ideal. You don't want a really lean grind. Your pie will be too dry.

Certain regions and countries have very specific ideas about meat pies. But I have no familial history with the meat pie. While my loyalties on this earth are many, they are not to the meat pie.

Perhaps there is a heralded meat pie in your region, or ethnicity. Pursue it. Look for recipes. Find stories about it in church cookbooks and third-shift bars. I can only offer the guidelines for a patty that tastes incredible. A classic meat patty is quite golden in color. If you desire that richness, use the double crust recipe with 2 tablespoons (14 g) of ground tumeric sifted into the dry ingredients and one egg mixed in with the crust.

Preheat the oven to 425°F (220°C, gas mark 7).

Filling

In a 8- or 10-inch (20 or 25 cm) cast iron or Dutch oven heat the olive oil and add the diced onion over medium heat. Once the onion becomes fragrant and translucent, turn the heat up to medium high and add the ground beef to brown. Break up the beef with a wooden spatula so it doesn't stay in a block and so the most surface area of the meat is exposed in the pan. Add the jalapeños and poblanos. I like this mixture of peppers; they combine to give a bit of heat and some taste. If you are about intense spice, opt for a Scotch bonnet pepper instead. Just make sure you use kitchen gloves as you deseed and cut it or you are in for a rude awakening.

Sauté for about 5 minutes and add the stock or beer and tablespoon of hot sauce. Season the meat with salt, pepper, and curry powder. Scatter the bread crumbs over the mixture and turn the pan on low. Stir occasionally over the next 15 or 20 minutes. The filling will become more solid as the bread crumbs absorb the fat and liquid while it also evaporates. It will be firm but moist. Taste for salt and pepper. Adjust if necessary. Finish with fresh, chopped thyme leaves and the zest and juice of one lime.

Let the filling cool. The fastest way to cool it is to spread it out on a baking sheet and refrigerate it.

Crust

Pull your crust out of the refrigerator and separate each disk into 3 equal-size balls. Roll each ball out in a circle as you would any other crust. Beat your egg for the wash and get your pastry cutter if you have one and a fork ready. Put ½ cup (112 g) of the chilled filling in the top third of the crust, leaving at least 1 inch (2.5 cm) of bare crust on the perimeter. Brush the edges of the crust with the egg wash and pull the bottom of the crust on top of the filling, making sure the edges meet. Press the edges together to seal the patty. Using a sharp knife or pasta cutter, trim the edges. Use the tines of a fork to seal the seam. Wash the outside of the crust with the egg wash. Put the patties on a baking sheet lined with parchment paper.

Meat patties are kind of like burritos; you want to put more filling in them than they can generally hold. An important objective is to make sure the edges are sealed, hence the egg wash, pressing, and fork tines. If your patty overrunneth, for whatever reasons, just pull out some of the filling.

Bake the patties for about 25 minutes, or until the crust is golden and crusty. Serve with whatever sauce you desire.

Yield: 6 patties

Jailhouse Cheesecake

For the crust

Box "gram" crackers

1 stick butter

For the filling

big cup of whipped topping

1½ cups granulated sugar

1 package (8 ounces) cream cheese, institutionalized brand, cell softened

¼ cup milk

Pie plate

Per Bilgren offers this cheesecake recipe that is the result of time spent in Rikers Island, the main jail complex for New York City located in the East River between Queens and the Bronx. This recipe is written on a cocktail napkin, which is in the direct spirit of people sharing recipes, or receipts as they were used to be called, on index cards. Beyond the ingenuity of what happens behind prison walls, really, we only hear about the terrible things, I am struck by a few things. Inmates are motivated enough to venture into icebox cooking in jail? The perseverance of the human spirit and appetite, in the face of hard time, is triumphant, and mainly I am struck by the following: They make their own pie crust in jail. For shame if you cannot muster the strength.

As transcribed from the napkin:

Melt the butter and crust the gram crackers or nilla wafers. Put around the pan. Then get whipped topping, 1 big cup, sugar, about 1½ cups, and cream cheese. Mix the cream cheese and whipped topping and a little milk and sugar. Mix real good and nice and fluffy. Then put in pan with your crust around it. Put it in a freezer for an hour and then in the fridge and you have a nice pie. Jailhouse.

Resources

Knowledge and Experience

The Brooklyn Kitchen
www.thebrooklynkitchen.com
Accessories, classes in the kitchen, private events

The Meat Hook
 www.the-meathook.com
*Aficionados of butchery and purveyors of the
highest quality beef, lamb, pork, and poultry*

Products

Daisy Flour
www.daisyflour.com
*100% organic premium flour available in whole
and whole wheat*

Anchor Hocking Company
www.anchorhocking.com
*A leading manufacturer of an all-inclusive line of
glass bakeware and glass products since 1905*

Le Creuset Cookware
www.lecreuset.com
*Exceptional quality cast iron cookware with a
porcelain enamel glaze and pie birds*

Lodge Cast Iron
www.lodgemfg.com
*Seasoned steel skillets for professional, camp, and
home use made in the U.S.*

KitchenAid
www.kitchenaid.com
*Great kitchen gadgets and small appliances,
including their signature stand mixer*

Books

The following books are instructional and
inspirational.

Au Pied de Cochon: The Album
by Martin Picard, Restaurant Au Pied de Cochon,
2006.

James Beard's American Cookery
by James Beard, Little Brown and Company, 1972.

The Best of Shaker Cooking
by Amy Bess Miller, Persis Fuller, William Whitehill,
and Beverly Hallock, Collier Books, 1993.

*Beyond Nose to Tail: More Omnivorous Recipes
for the Adventurous Cook*
by Fergus Henderson and Justin Piers, Bloomsbury,
USA, 2007

Couscous and Other Good Food from Morocco
by Paula Wolfert, Ecco; Perennial Library Ed. Edition,
1987.

English Bread and Yeast Cookery
by Elizabeth David, Penguin Cookery Library, 1977.

Forking Fantastic! Put the Party Back in Dinner Party
by Zora O'Neill and Tamara Reynolds
Gotham Books, 2009.

*Maryland's Way: The Hammond-Harwood
House Cookbook*
by Mrs. Lewis R Andrews and Mrs. J. Reaney Kelly
Hammond-Harwood House Association, 1966.

Mastering the Art of French Cooking
by Simone Beck, Louisette Bertholle, and Julia Child
Alfred A. Knopf, 1973.

My Life in France
by Julia Child and Alex Prud'Homme
Alfred A. Knopf, 2007.

*On Food and Cooking: The Science and Lore
of the Kitchen*
by Harold McGee, Scribner, 1984, 2004.

*Pie: 300 Tried-and-True Recipes for Delicious
Homemade Pie*
by Ken Haedrich, The Harvard Common Press, 2004.

*Ratio: The Simple Codes Behind the Craft of
Everyday Cooking*
by Michael Ruhlman, Scribner, 2009.

*The Raw and the Cooked: Adventures of a Roving
Gourmand*
by Jim Harrison, Grove Press, 2001.

The Whole Beast: Nose to Tail Eating
by Fergus Henderson, Ecco, 2004.

About the Author

Millicent Souris is a cook in Brooklyn, New York. She was born in Baltimore, Maryland, and early on showed an aptitude for animal husbandry and the Russian language. Neither took.

About the Photographer

Greg Vore is a commercial photographer who lives and works in Brooklyn, New York. He is a Taurus who loves BBQ, bourbon, and record collecting. This is his first cookbook.

Acknowledgments

First and foremost thanks to my mother Sally Snell and my sisters Maggi Souris and Molli Souris. You have all tapped into some unknown reserve of patience and support when it comes to me. The Brooklyn Kitchen and owners Harry Rosenblum and Taylor Erkkinen proved to be intensely generous, offering their kitchens for recipe testing and photography. Brooklyn Kitchen employees followed suit with their helpfulness and encouragement. Along the same lines, The Meat Hook and butchers Tom Mylan, Ben Turley, Brent Young, Sara Bigelow, and Matt Greene were charitable souls. Greg Vore is an amazing photographer, even with a set of busted up hands and arms like mine to work with, and Rebecca Collerton is a wonderful stylist with a great eye. There was a fair share of beg, borrow, and steal along the way. I am truly grateful to the people who offered recipes: Per Billgren, Eben Burr, Greta Dana, Ladleah Dunn, Julie Farias, Caroline Fidanza, Anne Fidanza, Kelly Geary, Annaliese Griffin, Jim Harrison, Caitlin Horsmon, Sophie Kamin, Tamara Reynolds, Nate Smith, and Michelle Warner. Much gratitude to the kind and hospitable souls at Saltie, Roebling Tea Room, Marlow and Daughters, Marlow and Sons, The Commodore, Dandelion Wine, Champion, and Troost. I am indebted to the charitable people of Daisy Flour and Anchor Hocking Company. Thank you for making such quality products in the USA.

Thank you, Rochelle Bourgault, for bringing me in off the streets and Betsy Gammons for taking care of me. The following people are important to acknowledge: Anna Dunn, Katy Porte, Liz Poirier, Cari Dolyniuk, Emily Flake, Bettina Richards, Ann Hruby, Annemarie Ahearn, Maggie Nesciur, Dennis Spina, Jaime Eldredge, Bobby Hellen, Elizabeth Schula, Marcy Roberts, Ian Christe, and Joyce Bahle. Thank you, Matt Stark, for the rocking chair, the leather cuff, and the inspiration. And thank you, for reading my book.

This book is dedicated to Dara Greenwald and Gerard Smith. We lost some good eaters, fantastic artists, and great people.

Index